Alexander Johnstone Wilson

Banking reform

An essay on prominent banking dangers and the remedies they demand

Alexander Johnstone Wilson

Banking reform
An essay on prominent banking dangers and the remedies they demand

ISBN/EAN: 9783337111380

Printed in Europe, USA, Canada, Australia, Japan

Cover: Foto ©Suzi / pixelio.de

More available books at **www.hansebooks.com**

AN ESSAY

ON PROMINENT BANKING DANGERS AND THE

REMEDIES THEY DEMAND

BY

ALEXANDER JOHNSTONE WILSON,

AUTHOR OF 'THE RESOURCES OF MODERN COUNTRIES.'

LONDON:

LONGMANS, GREEN, & CO.

1879

COLSTON AND SON, PRINTERS, EDINBURGH.

PREFACE.

THE following pages deal with some of the practical questions at issue in modern English Banking, and with these alone. They are of the highest importance at the present time, and yet signs are not wanting that the lessons which recent events might have been expected to teach are being to some extent forgotten. Bank directors have fixed their attention upon points which, however important to shareholders, do not touch the heart of the difficulty. All our banks, joint-stock and private, require to be reduced to order, to be protected against themselves.

Within less than a generation the modern deposit system has reached its present gigantic developments. Until the gold discoveries of California and Australia took place, we may indeed say that there was no gigantic bank in the country. But since 1858 the liabilities of many joint-stock banks, and of some private banks also, have more than doubled. And in all directions banks have extended their operations and altered their habits since the date of the misdirected legislation of Sir Robert Peel. The time has now come, therefore' when the Legislature ought to be prepared to bring the confused and even chaotic elements thus devoloped into something like order.

It is the aim of this essay to indicate briefly the main lines on which the necessary reforms ought to run ; and I may say that the views it contains are not put forward as altogether the expression of outside opinion. They have been much discussed with bankers in the City, and are to a considerable extent what the most enlightened among them feel to be necessary.

An essay written by me about a year ago, and printed in the *Fortnightly Review* for August last, has been reprinted as the first chapter of the volume, for the purpose of re-calling the minds of readers to the most wide-spread banking dangers of the time. The crash in Glasgow eclipsed many of these dangers which exist still, and can in no way be removed while losses in trade continue to accumulate. In short, we are not yet clear of danger ; and I fear, it must be added, not free from the dead weight of past losses, still hidden and unacknowledged to an extent that presses down enterprise and helps to prevent a real trade revival. The fact that so much rottenness overlays our credit and clogs our trade, is one additional reason for urging that all the banks of the country, joint-stock and private, should speedily be brought to book. If we leave them much longer, it may be too late for them and for the nation. But the dangers visible on all sides also offer powerful reasons against hasty legislation or anything like imperfect patching. To deal with the questions of limited and unlimited liability, or even to try to assimilate the law of Scotland in the matter of trustees holding stock to the provisions of the English 'Joint-Stock Companies Act of 1862,' might prove highly dangerous just at the moment. The very urgency of the reform demands that it should be carefully and deliberately brought about, and therefore the best course to be pursued, is probably one that would give the banks time to prepare themselves for great changes in the law. Were the Government to appoint a small carefully chosen Commission to inquire into the present state of banking with a view to legislation, it might be the wisest thing which in the circumstances it could do. The researches of such a body would do much preliminary good ; would furnish the basis of thorough legislation ; and would, at the same

time, give the banks opportunity for putting
their affairs in order against the day of compulsion. A step of this kind would not be
seriously resisted by the bankers. Some
among them might, perhaps, hope that an
investigation of the kind would procure an
indefinite respite from interference; and there
would be danger of that result were public
opinion to go to sleep upon the subject.
There is, however, less probability of that
being the case than some might suppose;
for while the present trade stagnation continues, banks will continue to fail from time
to time, and their collapse will keep public
feeling alive. All that we shall require,
therefore, is that this public feeling should
be utilised for a sound practical purpose;
and if the following observations contribute
in any degree to that result, my object in
writing will be fully attained.

LONDON, 25th February 1879.

CONTENTS.

---∞×⊙×∞---

CHAPTER I.

CHAPTER II.

CHAPTER III.

CHAPTER IV.

CHAPTER V.

CHAPTER VI.

CHAPTER VII.

BANKING REFORM.

————◆————

CHAPTER I.

THE POSITION OF ENGLISH JOINT-STOCK BANKS.*

FEW things are at present more striking than
the apparent extreme prosperity of the joint-
stock banks of this country. The complaints
as to dulness of trade have been universal
now for at least three years. You can hardly
pick up a trade circular or chairman's speech
at some half-yearly company meeting without
finding in it allusions to the depressed conditions of our national industries and the
unsatisfactory character of the profits. In the
iron and coal trades particularly, things have
gone from bad to worse. Some of the largest
smelting works in the country have ceased
to produce, and hundreds of smaller concerns
either work along in great distress or dis-
appear altogether, leaving little but debts to indicate that they ever existed. Prices in almost

* Reprinted from the *Fortnightly Review* for August 1878.

A

all departments of business have been falling
continuously for many months, and therefore,
although the bulk of the trade done may
have been in some cases nearly as large as
ever, it has often been trade conducted at a
loss. There is, in short, undeniable evidence
of strain everywhere, and business has in
consequence been contracted wherever possible
within the narrowest limits. We can hardly
put our finger upon an industry of any importance the country through, and say,—this
branch of trade at least is good ; unless we
consider the manufacture of instruments of
destruction worthy of being taken into account.
Sheffield languishes for lack of demands for
its cutlery ; Bradford is oppressed with an
excess of manufacturing power for the ' stuffs '
which have at present no free market ; Manchester warehouses are groaning beneath the
weight of unsold and at present unsaleable
cotton goods ; the sugar industry has almost
departed from Bristol ; and at nearly all centres
of our silk manufacture stocks accumulate and
prices sink. In the Black country the stagnation is nearly universal ; and even Birmingham hardware is not bought so freely as in
former years. Everywhere almost there are
at home signs of languishing, of the same
reaction from over-production, and these are

frequently aggravated by indications of increased foreign competition.

Such a state of things, one would naturally expect, must tell with instant force upon the position of our joint-stock banks. In their hands, for the most part, the trade of the country finds the means by which purchase and sale become possible. They have gathered the larger share of the surplus money possessed by the community into their hands, and have so developed the facilities for lending, for making and receiving payments, that the bulk of our trade hinges on them. We should, therefore, naturally suppose that if trade is languishing they would languish, and that only when it was active and yielding good profits would they prosper.

The case is, to all appearance, as near as may be just the reverse. If we except the London Joint-Stock Banks, to whose position further reference shall be made presently, the situation seems most prosperous. There is no diminution in dividends paid ; on the contrary, they are higher in some instances than they were before 1873—the year when our trade prosperity may be said to have culminated. Reserves increase, and deposits appear to flow in until one wonders what can be meant by complaints about bad trade,

declining profits, and industrial distress. So
steady is the apparent growth of prosperity
on the part of the country joint-stock banks in
particular, that they frequently find it necessary
to call up more capital in order to meet the
demands of an extended business, and large
dividends are paid on this capital with no
difficulty whatever. Thus we learn from the
Banker's Magazine for February last, that in
the two years, 1876 and 1877, the net increase
in the capital of the joint-stock banks of the
country was over £4,000,000, including the
premiums, in some cases very high, charged
on the new issues of shares and placed to
reserve funds, and the undivided profits also
placed to reserve. This, to be sure, appears
to include the Scotch and Irish banks, with
which we are not now dealing; but the
additions to capital made by them are small,
and the bulk of the increased capital is to
be credited to the joint-stock banks in England, mostly to those in the provinces. Of
course all this increase does not represent
money on which dividend is nominally paid,
the premium being added to the reserve, on
which there is no obligation to pay. But it
may be considered that a full half of it does;
and yet, as I have said, dividends do not fall
off, except in a few isolated instances. It is a

common enough event to find 20 and 22 per cent. per annum distributed on the paid-up capital, and anything under 10 per cent. is considered a very indifferent return.

I shall give a few averages for the last two years only in order to make this point evident, dividing the banks into (1) London banks proper; (2) London banks with provincial branches; (3) banks in provincial cities; and (4) banks having an important part of their business in agricultural districts. There are in the first category eight banks* in all, excluding the 'Metropolitan,' which does not pay a dividend on the whole of its capital, and is, in other respects, difficult to classify, and the average dividend paid to the shareholders of these eight banks during the last two years has been $10\frac{1}{2}$ per cent. per annum. This is a lower average than was customary just before the Collie frauds of 1875, the same eight banks having distributed in the years 1873 and 1874 an average dividend of fully $13\frac{1}{4}$ per cent. per annum, but it is none the less a remarkable yield.

In the second category we have five banks, excluding the Amalgamated Hampshire and North Wilts Bank, which has only recently

* The names of these eight banks will be found at the head of an abstract of their accounts further on.

come to London, and the Scotch and Irish
banks with city offices. These five banks—
the Consolidated, whose chief business is in
Manchester, the London and County, the
National Provincial, the London and Provincial,
and the London and South-Western—paid an
average dividend of almost 13½ per cent. per
annum in the two years 1875 and 1876, which
is much higher than the average of the London
banks proper for the same period, and shows
but little diminution upon the yield of the two
years 1873 and 1874, which was only 14 per
cent. per annum,

The third class of banks is a large one, and
in some cases difficult to separate from the more
distinctly rural banks. I have, however, taken
thirty-one banks whose centres of business are
in Birmingham, Liverpool, Manchester, Leeds,
Sheffield, Bradford, Halifax, and such like
trading and manufacturing districts, and, avoid-
ing those which have a considerable number of
rural branches, have endeavoured to strike an
average which shall tolerably closely represent
the earnings of provincial city banks in the
past two years. This average I find to be
about 14 per cent. per annum; the dividends
ranging from a mere 5 per cent., as in the case
of the Nottingham Joint-Stock Bank, to the 30
per cent. paid by the Lancaster Bank. Con-

sidering the variety of conditions under which these banks carry on business, this average is remarkable, apart altogether from the question whether trade is dull or active. It shows that these banks, like the London banks with provincial branches, have large sources of revenue, and the condition of banking in provincial towns would appear at first sight to be much more favourable than in the city of London itself. No doubt the high dividend is in many instances paid on a relatively smaller paid-up capital than some of the London banks possess; but the country banks are in numerous instances facing increased disadvantages in this respect compared with those of London, inasmuch as they are the banks which we find continually augmenting their paid-up capital. They are doing this, it would seem, with impunity in the meantime, and in only a few instances are the dividends paid for the last two years lower than those paid for the previous two years. Where this does occur, too, it is in the case of banks which have not added to their capital. Here also we have, therefore, an appearance of prosperity which is remarkable, explain it how we may.

But this prosperity is, if possible, more striking still in the case of the banks I have selected as rural banks, that is, which do a large business in

purely agricultural districts. Of these I have
picked out twenty-nine, taking them, as in the
previous list, alphabetically from the list given
in the *Investor's Monthly Manual*, and omitting
only one or two very small banks, about whose
rural connection I am doubtful. These twenty-
nine banks have yielded an average dividend,
for the last two years, whose figures have been
published, of about 16 per cent. per annum.
Some of them have not, up to the time of this
writing, announced their dividend for the past
year, so that the average does not compare
strictly on all fours with the others. But here
also the indications of falling dividends are few,
and almost counterbalanced by instances in
which the payment has been higher than in
previous years. Such banks as the Yorkshire,
the Wilts and Dorset, the Hampshire and
North Wilts, the North and South Wales, and
the Bury banks, pay steady dividends of from 17
to 25 per cent. with the greatest regularity and
ease in the world; and, as a result, we have a
general average for banks which we may consider at least partially rural, higher than for either
banks in manufacturing districts or in London.

These figures are altogether startling, unless
we could prove that the banks have taken
advantage of the uncertainties of the trading
community to exact higher terms for the money

they lend. The superficial facts appear, however, to prove just the contrary, for the nominal value of money or the price of credit has seldom been so low as it has been in this country, and on every great money market in the world, since 1875. When bill brokers are thankful to discount good paper at the rate of $\frac{3}{4}$ per cent. per annum, as they have more than once been within the past three years, we can hardly say off-hand that banking profits have been made out of dearer credit. What makes the dividend averages we have given still more remarkable, is the curious increased ratio which they bear to the degree of prosperity enjoyed by the regions within scope of their operations. Thus, while the London banks pay a comparatively low average dividend, in spite of the greater scope for business which they enjoy even in dull times, the banks with agriculture connections pay the highest rate of all. Now agriculture has been an unprofitable occupation for years past in this country. We have had at least two bad harvests in succession; rents are nearly everywhere so unreasonably high, that in many instances landowners have been driven to relieve their tenants by making large reductions, and have frequently had farms left on their hands, because in times so bad no tenant would face the rent responsibility. Foreign

competition in the supply of food of all kinds
has at the same time been on the increase, and
the farmers' old compensation for a bad year
—high prices—can no longer be secured.   He
has thus nothing to relieve him from the full
pressure of landlord monopoly and bad times.
Yet, in spite of all this, the rural banks pay
most flourishing dividends.   How is all this to
be accounted for?

To answer this question thoroughly, I should
have to institute an examination of some length
into the principles now supposed to govern
English banking.   In my view, few subjects
are at present of more vital interest to the
community, but I do not propose to enter at
any length into such a discussion now.   My
object is rather to lay bare the immediate and
visible causes of the apparent prosperity of
our joint-stock banks than to examine the
principles of banking in the abstract, and I
shall therefore rest content with a reference
to one or two general considerations which
serve to show that, within certain limits, dull
trade is, fairly enough, not without its compensations to the banker.   This I shall do chiefly
with a view to bring into greater relief the
dangerous practices with which banks have
so often cked out those compensations in times
like the present.

And first of all it must be remembered that, apart from the fact that nearly all banks earn interest on more money than the amount of their paid-up capital, dear or cheap money makes very little difference to the amount of profits they can get on a certain more or less important portion of their balances.   Those banks whose 'deposits' are large, can count on merely a margin between what they pay for the use of these deposits and what they can earn by them, whether the value of money be high or low.   When money is dear, the depositors ask a larger interest on their balances, and 'when it is cheap they must perforce accept a lower.   The banks get merely the difference.   Hence, if they can employ the money at all, their profits may be almost as much on this class of balance when the Bank of England value of money is low as when it is high.   Of course the floating balances on which no interest is paid will not yield so much, and in that respect the banks of large current account resources will stand at a disadvantage, a fact which no doubt helps to explain the lower earning power of the London banks in recent years.   These also suffer severely from another and more per-manent cause, inasmuch as they are subjected to much greater competition now than in

former years by the large number of colonial,
foreign, and Scotch banks whose offices in
the City draw away from the City banks
proper much business and money.

Another general consideration, which relates
rather more to country banks than to metropolitan, is this : the ruling monetary rate quoted
in the bill market or by the Bank of England,
is to a considerable extent a fiction, because
it is, for one thing, based upon a false standard
of value.   Custom has sanctified the usage
which compels all banks to follow the Bank
of England in its movement of the 'rate for
money.'   There is no real ground for this
custom, and it does frequently as much harm
as good, because the Bank of England is often
moved by causes peculiar to itself, whether in
raising or lowering this rate.   The market
rate is thus sometimes above and often below
that of the Bank of England, and that bank is
frequently compelled to place itself 'out of the
market' by a high rate, merely that it may
protect the national store or reserve of bullion.
But be this practice wise or the reverse, we
should never forget that it is a practice which
roughly determines the value of money for
first-class merchants' or bankers' bills alone.
It does not establish, and only in a remote
degree influences, the rate charged throughout

the provinces for second-class bills or for advances with or without security. Even in London there is an enormous mass of small bill discounting done at 5 or 6 per cent. when the nominal Bank of England rate may be only 2 per cent., and the open market rate for the best paper barely half as much. This is not usurious discounting either, but the ordinary fate of fair trade bills, drawn probably by City merchants on the small retailers. In this class of business a time of so-called 'cheap money' is consequently a time of high profits, for the banker is paying little for his deposits and getting much for their use, at the same time that the presence of dull trade is perhaps driving more of this kind of bills into the market. Throughout the provinces, where the bills circulating are on the average smaller than in London, this fixity of discount rate is of course much more customary, and the natural inference would be that in a time of dull trade banks could make a very good profit, provided always that they found steady employment for all their money. It is true, no doubt, that joint-stock banks in the country do not reap the full advantage of the difference between what they earn on money in times like these and what they pay for it, because they have probably always to pay rather more for their deposits than London bankers now do. The Bank of England rate is more a fiction with them at all times than it is in London, and their standard for interest payment on deposits is rather the yield on consols than 'bank' rate. If they cannot allow some 3 per cent. on the money entrusted to them, their customers place it in the funds, so they are probably compelled in the dullest of times to pay about so much for the use of money. This is, however, only a partial drawback, as they are, on the other hand, able to command a higher price for their credits and discountings, and as these may tend to increase in bad times, their earnings are to a certain extent also legitimately higher. ·

These general observations might be assumed to have almost settled the point, did we not know that banking nowadays means much more than a mere discounting of bills. This is indeed but a small branch of the business of many banks, and in order to obtain some just conception of the position into which a period of dull business has brought them, I must now ask the reader's indulgence while I plunge into one or two statements of principles and figures. I shall try not to overload my pages with the latter, but a few are absolutely necessary.

Bankers nowadays are subjected to enormous temptations to travel beyond the line of their safe legitimate business, which may be briefly described as the business of borrowing for short periods on the security of their capital, in order to lend again for short periods upon mercantile securities at a profit. Their chief resources should thus be always *floating*. A banker has no business, for example, to lend money on the mortgage of a house which may not be realisable should necessity arise for calling in his money, and though less questionable, perhaps, the habit of lending on stocks and shares may also turn out to be an extremely dangerous one. But stocks and shares and house property of all descriptions have multiplied so fast in recent years that the temptation to the banker to take these as 'security' for loans made with his customers' money has proved irresistible. He lends heavily on such in brisk times, helps to 'float' loans, backs adventures in railways, mining, house - building, and navigation on all hands, and in innumerable ways steps aside from his true position as mere go-between and auxiliary in ordinary commercial transactions, while in times of bad trade the temptation to make profit by such business is not to be resisted.

It may be justly said that a bank which

allows itself to be drawn largely into speculations of any kind, involving great difficulty in
the sudden realisation of its money, is a bank
which, if it does not ultimately fail altogether,
must suffer grievous loss.   It is wise to invest
guarantee funds in approved home securities,
and it may be at times prudent to place a
portion of the paid-up capital in the same
position, but it is never safe for a bank to
put any money belonging to customers into
any security which is not continually, as it were,
realising itself, a security where the risks of
loss are small, and, comparatively speaking,
immediate.   This I believe to be the one
cardinal principle of sound banking ; and now
let us examine the present position of English
joint-stock banks in relation thereto.

The task is less easy than it might seem,
owing to the careless or indifferent fashion in
which all joint-stock banks draw up their
balance-sheets.   I have found the greatest
difficulty in collecting the facts indicated in the
statements of the various categories of banks
whose figures I have examined, simply because
these figures are often for practical purposes
of no use at all.   What shall be said, for
example, of the practice which heaps all the
items of a bank balance-sheet—-cash, securities, advances, bills, property, and overdrawn

accounts, into a lump sum! Nobody can tell
in the least how such an institution stands, yet
this is the common practice with many provincial joint-stock banks. And where some
details are given, they are rarely or ever
minute enough to enable one to tell even
approximately what the true position of an
institution may be. 'Cash in hand' and
'cash lent at call or notice' are, for example,
habitually lumped together, although the latter
involves a risk of loss while the former does
not ; bills, advances, and over-drafts are also
continually to be found swelling the sum total :
and country banks, never, so far as I can discover, indicate that portion of their liabilities
which represents the mere *contra* of unsecured
advances on current accounts ; nor is there
a bank within the United Kingdom which
separates its liability on deposits bearing
interest from the mere credit balances on
current accounts, although the former is a
liability of a kind quite distinct from the latter.
A great reform is needed in this respect, but
we shall probably have to wait for it till after
the next collapse of banking credit in this
country.   Then with our usual zealous endeavour to redress wrongs and retrieve blunders,
we will set vigorously to work to devise a
perfect credit-checking machine when it is

too late. The Government now looks after insurance companies, and compels them to publish returns, which have at least the advantage of indicating whether an office is extravagant or the reverse. Why should it not compel all joint-stock banks to publish balance-sheets which should at least enable the public to follow the changes which are continually taking place in the position of their accounts, and to see the character of their risks?

I shall leave that question to answer itself, and proceed to make the best of such figures as I have been able to procure, dealing first with those of the London banks. What strikes one most forcibly at first sight about these is the large decrease which has taken place in both their assets and liabilities between the end of 1873 and the end of 1877, the period which I have throughout chosen for comparison. I subjoin a table which will make this clear.

London Banks Proper — Alliance, Central, City, Imperial, Joint-Stock, Westminster, Merchants', Metropolitan, and Union — Increases or Decreases in their Working Resources and Liabilities.

ASSETS.

Cash in hand and at call, - £620,849 Net	{	Smaller banks, except City and Westminster, show increase.
Discounts and advances, - 10,395,314 Net	{	Smaller banks again show increase.
Securities, . - 186,123		

£11,202,276 Net decrease in the assets.

CAPITAL AND RESERVES.

Capital,	+	£5,002	In Metropolitan alone.
Reserves,	+	16,754	{ Heavy decrease in London and Westminster, small in Union, the rest all increases.

LIABILITIES TO THE PUBLIC.

Deposits,	−£9,029,944	Again increase in the smaller banks.
Acceptances,	− 2,463,685	{ Only Alliance and Metropolitan show increase; Joint-Stock and Central do not give their acceptances separately, but it is fair to assume that there has been a considerable falling off.
£11,493,629		Total decrease in the liabilities.

These banks, it will be seen, have lost no less than £9,000,000 of their deposit in four years, and there has been a falling off afterwards of £10,000,000 in their discounts and advances. This, at first sight, seems a reduction out of proportion to the falling off in the dividends, inasmuch as it is equal to about a tenth of their total resources in deposits and acceptances; but to some extent, no doubt, the loss of deposits was a relief. The banks are to that extent delivered from the burden of money which they could not profitably use, and for much of which they had to pay interest. Their own action has, indeed, to some degree caused this reduction in their balance-sheet totals; for since they ceased to give interest on current account balances, the tendency of these balances has been to grow narrower. This, however, is not the chief cause of the change,

much being due to the withdrawal of money
by country banks.

And what of the actual diminution in the
business done, as indicated by the decrease of
£10,000,000 in their discounts and advances?
The figures do not give details enough to
enable us to trace what this reduction consists
in, but there is strong reason for believing that
a paucity of trade bills and the keen competition
already mentioned are the main causes.   It is
noticeable that the item 'acceptance' is less
by about two millions and a half, and that reduction should represent a decrease in pure
mercantile business.   Naturally, moreover, the
more provident banks would curtail their advances on stocks, dock warrants, and other
securities, in proportion as they lost their
deposits, whether by their own free will, by
the competition of other banks, or by the
steady withdrawal of resources by the provincial banks, for whom the London banks act
as agents.   This last cause of reduction in the
working resources of the London banks has
been a most constant and powerful one, as
we shall see when we come to examine the
position of provincial banks.

On the whole, it may be safely concluded
that the reduction in the available resources
of the London banks, where they have not

been caused by losses pure and simple, like
the losses of the London and Westminster
Bank in the Collie and other frauds, has not
been an unmixed evil so far as their profits
are concerned. Their stability ought certainly
to be greater now than it was before. Unwieldy
masses of capital are most dangerous possessions
in times of mercantile depression. Could we
then be sure that these banks have no hidden
troubles, no safes full of bad or doubtful securities, no dangerously-extended credits, or deep
involvements with mercantile firms whose trade
is but a more or less frantic endeavour to
retrieve the losses of the past, we should say
their position is fairly sound and good. But
these are just the points upon which no man
can be sure until it has been seen how the
banks pass through the first ordeal of very dear
credit which shall succeed the depression of the
past few years.

I must now ask the reader to look at the
following table, giving an analysis of four
London banks with provincial branches,
similar to that given of the London banks
alone. The figures of the National Provincial,
now probably the largest bank in the kingdom,
were, when this was written, only available up
to the 31st December 1877; I shall therefore
deal with them separately :—

Comparative Statistics of London Banks with Provincial Branches (four banks, Consolidated, London and County, London and Provincial, London and South-Western).

ASSETS.

Cash, .	+£1,071,068	All show increases.
Advances, +	603,874	London and County alone decrease.
Securities, +	1,552,256	All increases.
	£3,227,198	Net increase in assets.

CAPITAL AND RESERVE.

Capital, . . +	£386,920	Consolidated no change.
Rest, . +	288,921	{ All increases, chiefly premiums on new shares.
	£675,841	

LIABILITIES TO THE PUBLIC.

Deposits,	+£6,531,953	All increases.
Acceptances,–	1,968,744	{ The London and Provincial does not state acceptances separately.
	£4,563,209	Net increase in liabilities.

These figures are remarkably in contrast to those of the London banks proper. The resources of these banks are greater instead of less, and they would seem to have considerable difficulty in finding use for the money entrusted to them. Their cash on hand and lent at call has increased by over £1,000,000 in the four years, and it is clear that they find great difficulty in employing their money in discount, for the principal increase in their assets is under the heading 'securities,' and their acceptances are very much reduced. Amongst them, these four banks now hold no less than £3,800,000 worth of stock, independently of the amounts pawned to them by customers as security for advances, and of which no indication is given. The London and County is driven most extensively to find this kind of employment for its money, and has at the present time some £800,000, more than its capital and reserve together, locked up in investments. But the figures of the National Provincial Bank of England are the most striking of all. This bank has now deposits amounting to upwards of £26,000,000, and its money invested in stocks probably exceeds £8,000,000 at the present date by a good round sum. At the date of the 1877 balance-sheet the total investments was nearly £7,500,000, and this is how that balance-sheet compares with 1873, or three years before.

THE NATIONAL PROVINCIAL BANK OF ENGLAND.

Comparative Figures of the Balance-Sheet, 1873-1876.

ASSETS.

Cash, ...	+	£553,141
Discount and advance,	+	2,841,982
Securities, . . .	+	2,204,290
Total increase,		£5,599,413

CAPITAL AND RESERVE.

Capital, . . .	+	£255,047
Rest, ...	+	300,000
Total increase,		£525,047

LIABILITIES TO THE PUBLIC.

Deposits, . . .	+	£5,026,101
Acceptances, . .	+	153,036
Total increase,		£5,179,137

Here again we see that the increase in the
resources of this bank has driven it more and
more to seek a profitable use for its money in
investments in stocks. Nearly half the increase in its deposits has gone in that direction,
and thus, were we able to say what proportion
of the £17,000,000 odd credited by it to
'discounts and advances,' was mercantile bills,
what advances on various kinds of securities
and pawned stocks, we should probably see
still more clearly how the great volume of
business which this bank does is sustained and
profitable. Although the acceptances of the
bank are rather more, the increase by no means
leads to the inference that mere mercantile
business is flourishing in the provinces though
stagnant in London. At the best we can only
infer that this bank has succeeded in drawing
to itself a better share of such good banking
business as is to be had.

If the reader will bear the infliction of a few
more figures relating to the provincial banks
alone, we shall see evidence in plenty that
mercantile bills of all kinds are not on the
increase. In this case the balance-sheets published vary from a mere statement of profits
to details regarding cash, discounts, advances,
etc., such as London banks do not give. The
diversity compels me therefore to dispense

with tables of figures, for I am unable to get a broad enough basis for comparison. There will be no difficulty, however, in arriving at some fair estimate of the position of the country banks by a strict analysis of the figures of the isolated balance-sheets taken from various parts of the country. I have worked out the results of some thirty of these, and find them to be so striking as to require almost no elucidation.

Four things, for instance, stand out prominently in the comparisons of the balance-sheets of the years 1873 and 1877 : (1) an unprecedented increase in the 'advances' to customers, upon security or on mere current account; (2) a heavy decrease in the amounts of trade bills held by the banks ; (3) a decrease in the available cash; and (4) an increase in the capital and reserve. A fifth feature might be added in the shape of an increase in the stocks held, but that is almost a necessary offset to the falling off in the trade bills and the increase in the deposits, as also, perhaps, to the extension in the advances.

The augmentation in the advances of customers is often very startling. For example, Lloyd's Banking Company and the Birmingham Joint-Stock Bank have increased this item in their balance-sheets by no less than £1,900,000 since 1873, and at the same time

their discounts have fallen away £697,000.
The position of Bradford, Manchester, and
Liverpool banks appears to be the same, so
far as I am able to trace their figures. And
this, at all events, is certain, that wherever
'advances' are stated separately, they show
unprecedented increases. It is the same too
with banks that may be considered partly as
agricultural. Thus I find that the Leicester-
shire Bank has increased its advances £459,000,
its discounts being lower by £99,000, while
Parr's Banking Company, in the same way, has
extended its credits by £1,122,000, while its
bills have fallen off £137,000. The Yorkshire and the Manchester City and County
yield indications of the same kind, and it is
only reasonable to conclude that in other instances, where the figures are too confused to
enable me to draw a sharply defined conclusion,
the larger totals are due to this identical
process.

Now, while this expansion of credit has been
going on for the past four years, the cash of
these banks has been diminishing, and some
of them have at the same time been making
repeated and extensive calls upon their shareholders for more capital. Taking capital and
reserves together, I find that eighteen provincial banks, out of some twenty whose balance-

sheets I have compared for the purpose, have
increased their resources in this way by upwards of £2,500,000 in the four years. Of
this total only a million is due to augmented
reserves, a full half of which may safely be
placed to the credit of premiums on share
issues, so that we may say £2,000,000 has been
added within the past four years to the paid-
up capital of some eighteen banks alone out of
the one hundred and twenty joint-stock banks
altogether in England and Wales. It is hardly
fair, perhaps, to take this as a sample of the
average increase, seeing that there are a
number of banks which have not resorted to
this practice; but granted that only pushing
banks in large business centres have thus acted,
the necessity for calling up such large sums of
money is surely very significant. They have
found a use for the money, without doubt, because it is all employed, and they are now, it
would seem, in need of more, but none the
less is the circumstance peculiar and worthy
of remark.

What, then, is the meaning of all these
changes in the accounts of the banks? The
key to it is very simple on the whole, and will
be found, I believe, for the most part in an explanation of the apparent growth in the total
liabilities of the banks on current and deposit

accounts, for these also have swollen with few exceptions. At first sight the figures of this increase seem very satisfactory. This bank and that has increased its liability on deposits, etc., *i.e.*, has to all appearance obtained money from its customers to the amount of a million, half million, or a few hundred thousands, more than it had four years ago. What could be more prosperous or more remarkable as a sign of the inherent soundness of the wealth of the country ? The country banks, in short, appear to be in many instances overburdened with an excess of money.

Unhappily the reverse of this pleasing picture gives the true facts. The banks are not bursting with deposits, they are very poor, and their customers are very poor. So poor are the latter that they have had to come to the banks again and again for advances of cash, in order to carry on their trade—too often a losing trade—and it is these advances which swell the totals on the debit side of 'deposit and current accounts.' These seeming large increases in the deposits are, in other words, merely cross entries. A customer of a bank gets, say, a loan of £10,000 on 'current account,' *i.e.* is allowed to overdraw to that amount with or without security, and the bank immediately credits his account with the over-draft, which then appears in the balance-sheet of the bank as a 'liability on current and deposit account.' No practice could be more misleading than that which wraps up these advances in this fashion ; but it is the fashion, nevertheless, and hence we see the curious phenomena of paucity of cash, increased capital and smaller discounts accompanying an apparent swelling of the deposits and available resources of these banks.*

* Up to the time of the City of Glasgow Bank failure the writer was subjected to much criticism in banking circles over this paragraph. It was asserted that a bank could not possibly make its balance-sheet up in the manner therein suggested. Since the revelations in Glasgow, this kind of criticism has died out, but I am nevertheless willing to admit that, without 'cooking' other parts of the balance-sheet, the plan of swelling the figures here suggested could not be easily carried out. That it can be done is, however, now beyond a doubt.

There is, however, another and fully as objectionable method of swelling the totals of a bank balance-sheet, to which I may as well advert here, as the rest of this volume deals, for the most part, with other phases of this large banking question. I allude to the practice, not uncommon among country bankers, of rediscounting their bills in London, and putting the money obtained from such rediscounts or 'pawning' amongst their deposits. By this means the figures of the balance-sheet may be swollen considerably, and the bank be made to appear wonderfully prosperous when it really is not so. For example, take a bank which is actually due to its depositors and customers, say £3,000,000, and which uses say £2,000,000 of this in discounting bills. In the ordinary course its balance-sheet would show on one side liabilities on current and deposit accounts, £3,000,000 ; and on the other bills discounted, £2,000,000, the rest of the money being either in hand or lent at call or on stocks. But the bank re-discounts £1,500,000 of its bills, and immediately invests the money so obtained in fresh bills. It may do this once or many times. If the bank does it only once, its balance-sheet would,

Of course, for a time, this practice seems very profitable. In all probability the banks lending in this way do not charge less than 5 per cent. interest, and 1 per cent. commission on the amount of the overdrawn accounts. They may often charge more, and each half-year the profits thus shown are added up and distributed as a big dividend to the shareholders. A further call on capital account is then made at a large premium, in order to provide further means for supporting these credits, and all goes swimmingly. But these banks are not, therefore, rich or sound; they may be just the reverse. Several of them are, indeed, at the present moment strained to the utmost to keep afloat, and it will, of course, depend on the nature of the securities they hold whether or not they can ultimately weather the storm which such financing is sure to breed.

The practice of thus dividing profits, which are in many instances nothing else than accretions to the debts due by their customers, is the exact financial counterpart of what a

according to custom, be made as follows:—To liability on current, deposit, and other accounts, £4,500,000 ; by bills discounted, £3,500,000. According to the length that this kind of doubling is carried will be the totals shown on both sides. It is needless to say that this kind of balance-sheet making is about as delusive as any that could be devised, and yet it is common enough.

railway company does when it credits itself with interest on capital advanced to tributary lines, and distributes dividends upon this credit, although the lines may not have paid a penny of the money. I remember an instance of a company which did this at a time when the worked lines were not paying their working expenses, and the company came to grief in consequence. Some of the joint-stock banks appear to be coming perilously near this kind of *denouement*.

I shall illustrate the situation by an example. Without giving their names, I take the balance-sheets of two banks, one urban, and one with agricultural business, and combining their figures, place them before the reader:—

Abstract of the Combined Balance-Sheets of two Country Joint-Stock Banks.

ASSETS.

	1873.	1877.		
Cash,	£1,623,000	. . £1,406,000	. . −	£217,000
Securities, .	212,000	. . 1,073,000	. . +	861,000
Bills discounted,	2,840,000	. . 2,114,000	. . −	726,000
Advances to customers,	2,171,000	. . 4,747,000	. . +	2,576,000
Total,	£6,840,000	. . £9,340,000	Net increase,£2,904,000	

LIABILITIES.

	1873.	1877.		
Deposits, credits on current account, etc.,	£6,095,000	. . £8,112,000	. . +	£2,017,000
Capital and reserves,	625,000	. . 1,206,000	. . +	581,000
Total,	£6,720,000	. . £9,318,000	. Increase, £2,598,000	

I have omitted minor items, such as the cost of bank offices, current profits, etc., and have

given only the bare skeleton of the balance-
sheets. The figures are in truth sufficiently
startling. Every available resource of these
banks is absorbed in maintaining the swollen
credits into which they have been drawn, and
even were we to take the £8,000,000 of liabilities to the public at the end of last year as
all real liabilities, which they are not—a large
proportion being obviously the cross entry
of advances representing, perhaps, the trade
losses or locks-up of their customers—the
position is not nearly so satisfactory now as
it was four years ago. It will be seen that
the apparent increase in the sum due to the
public under various heads approximates to
the augmentation in the advances, and that
these advances, together with the more extended investment in stocks, absorb the increase
in capital and the money set free by the diminished bill discounts, besides trenching on the
cash in hand.

In judging of the soundness or otherwise of
a bank, we have first of all to consider what
proportion its most available assets bear to the
liabilities. These assets are the cash and the
trade bills discounted—the actual money, and
the security most easily convertible into money
immediately and without loss, or which is always in the ordinary course of business con-

verting itself. If trade bills are good they should be equal to cash, less the price of discount, however bad the times. Now, in 1873, the cash and bills of those two banks amounted to upwards of 73 per cent. of the liabilities to the public, but at the end of last year they were equal to but about $43\frac{1}{2}$ per cent. These banks have therefore locked up their capital and available assets to an enormous extent in advances, and in stock which may or may not be realisable. Now these balance-sheets may, I believe, be taken as representative of a state of things which prevails all over the land, and the explanation of which is that although trade has been bad in nearly all its branches, merchants have gone on buying and selling, and the banks have hitherto sustained them under the losses incident to a narrower and a falling market. Farmers have suffered from short crops and low prices, and they in turn have been helped by their bankers in the hope that a better time will come when high profits will permit losses to be recouped. Manufacturers have kept their mills running in order to be ready for a revival of trade when it came. Miners have continued their output in the same way, and the net upshot of it all has been constantly falling prices and dwindling resources. The banks are therefore choked

with pawned securities of all kinds—stocks and
shares, mortgages on property, on manufactured
goods, on raw produce, and are under advances
without security in cases innumerable. The
losses of the community from those and other
causes have thus so far been buried in the
banks. In all probability a large proportion
of the advances which they have continued to
make in this fashion will never be fully recovered,
and the day may, therefore, be not far distant
when many a bank shareholder may have to
pay back the high profit he has enjoyed all
through the years of depressed trade in calls to
fill up yawning deficits which cannot otherwise
be made good.

It may be said that the amount of bills and
cash should not be taken as the only readily
available resource possessed by the banks.
Many of the securities they hold are good
and realisable, and ought therefore to be
included in the assets which could be turned
to account at a pinch. This is no doubt true
in a sense, but even if we allow that the
banks might be able to realise their Consols,
for example, on an emergency, the position
would not be materially altered. Consols
form, in the majority of cases, the smallest
of the securities which banks in this position
hold, and it would be impossible to find a

market even for Consols were many banks pressed to sell at the same time. Outside themselves there would be few buyers, and amongst those disposed to buy few could find the means without that banking assistance which, in a time of financial strain, is sure to be wanting. The truth of the matter is, as I insisted at the outset, that it is not in the long run prudent banking to lock up in mere stock exchange securities any portion of money which is liable at any time to be called for by its owners. That money ought to be in bills, in securities which represent commodities continually changing hands and undergoing realisation, securities which are therefore continually bringing the money back again to the banker's hands. If through dearth of these, or from any other cause, a banker buys interest-bearing stock to large amounts, or lends money on such stock pawned with him as security, he at once places himself in the position of having to face indefinite losses in the event of a forced realisation. He cannot always be sure of being able to realise when he wants to, and the more widespread the lock-up in such stocks the greater the difficulty of sale—the more certain the ultimate loss. For a banker by employing money entrusted to him in holding stocks contributes most

materially to inflate the value of those stocks.
The demand thus created is not natural, the
outcome of private investment, but artificial,
and the result is artificial prices which tell
at once against the banker when his selling
day comes. Especially is this the case where
the price of certain kind of credit is abnor-
mally low, for then the customers of a bank
are only too ready to employ their deposit
money in the same way, partly as 'cover'
for stocks bought and pawned with a view
to secure a higher rate of interest than the
banker chooses to allow. I cannot admit,
therefore, that the position of those banks
which have placed large sums of money out
on advances, or into stock investment, is
intrinsically sound, or that the test of bills
and cash applied to their ability to meet
engagements is other than a just one. But
if one can hardly believe in the soundness
of the banking which puts customers' money
largely out into stocks, what shall be said
of the immense credits which have been
granted on the security of real estate, the
huge loans on building speculations, the
pawned leases and the innumerable instances
where money has been advanced on personal
security only ? Can the banks stand a strain
of credit with all these on their back ? With-

out calling upon their shareholders I am
sure that many of them cannot, and these
imprudent commitments are in many instances alone sufficient to imperil the position of
banks which now enjoy abundant credit and
the repute of good management.

It is to be noticed, moreover, that even the
strict test which I have applied is to some
extent a deceptive one, so far at least as
regards the 'cash,' for the figures which
appear in the half-yearly balance-sheets by
no means represent the actual state of the
till throughout the rest of the year. We
know from the sharpness with which loans
are called in just before the balance is
struck, that many banks make a regular practice of providing for a good show at the half-
year's end, and consequently we may justly
infer that much more money is in some shape
out of hand throughout the year than appears
in the balance-sheet. Now money out on
loan, even for a day, is money risked, and the
barer banks keep their tills of cash, the
greater the danger of sudden demands which
a market by no means well supplied might
be unable to meet. A process of denudation
has been going on in respect to the cash at
the best, which the fictitiously low rate for
bill discounts in London has served to conceal.

Country banks have, as we have noted, withdrawn much of their balances from the hands
of their London agents, in order to help their
country customers, and everywhere the disposition has been to work on as narrow a
cash basis as possible. The Bank of England
has been for some time gradually losing its
store of gold, and its reserve of notes is at
present hardly £11,000,000 with the discount
rate at 2½ per cent., and a liability on the part
of the banks to the public of probably not
less than £500,000,000, including the deposits
in private banks. If, therefore, the little cash
that banks do show in their balance-sheets,
when compared with their liabilities to the
public and with the balance-sheets of four
years ago, is to a considerable extent in the
hands of bill-brokers, stock-brokers, speculators
of all kinds throughout the year, may we not
say that the position is beyond measure a
dangerous one? It is bolstering all round.
A fictitious level of value is maintained on
mere windy credit, and when a pressure
comes, tending to make things find their
real level, there will be great danger of a
general collapse. The cash which banks hold
at the half-year's end is not their true available store all the year round. For the year,
all but four or five days, they may run

much shorter of mere till-money than their balance-sheets reveal, and they do in fact so run. It will be said that this is surely a stupid and self-deluding way of conducting business, and no doubt it is, but so long as banks are permitted to publish such balance-sheets as they please, and when they please, it is a practice that cannot be rooted out.

In this view of the situation, nothing could well seem more absurd than the nominally low value of money; but the position of the joint-stock banks enables us to see without difficulty how it has been brought about. There are in fact two values of money ruling, as it were, side by side: one a matter of bargain between borrower and lender—the private loan made with or without security, for which the interest charged has been high—and the other, the open market rate for bills of exchange of the highest class. These latter have been a dwindling quantity, and as they have fallen off more rapidly than the surplus cash obtained by the bankers either from customers or shareholders was absorbed by the private lending and stock-jobbing, the interest obtainable for their negotiation has receded to a very low figure. But this low figure is no test whatever of the scarcity or abundance of money, except as regards its employment in a particular way, and hence the supplies of real cash kept in hand by bankers have been dwindling almost everywhere, at the same time that the floating balance available for discount purposes has been almost valueless. Banks are thus drifting towards a catastrophe, one may almost say without being aware of it. They have striven to make high profits in dull times and in channels not safe for bankers, and they have succeeded, but at a cost which only those who survive the next credit storm will be able to estimate.

That a storm of this kind is coming, I think there can be not the least doubt, and we can tell pretty clearly how it will come. Had this country rushed into war and begun to call up large sums of money on loan, that would have brought on a financial crisis almost at once. But it will come not less surely, though not perhaps so soon, should the world once more settle down to an uncomfortable armed peace. Trade will in that event make an effort at revival. It is showing some signs of life in this country now, but these, I think, are merely spasmodic—an outcome in part of the eager haste with which the Government spent most of its £6,000,coo. Still trade will wake up a little now that peace is concluded, and with its

revival there will be an immediate pressure on
the floating capital in bankers' hands. More
bills for large amounts will be drawn and
offered for discount, and directly these reach
a certain volume the bankers will find themselves without money to conduct their proper
business.   An effort will then be made to sell
some of the securities held, or loans will be
called in, involving sharp losses, and attempts
will be made to get rid of mortgages, all with
a view to find money for trade purposes.   This
will in the first place produce a heavy fall in
stock exchange securities, and may induce
something like a panic. Banks will then in
some cases have either to face losses, or to hold
on to their securities and trust to weathering
the storm, and the pressure for money may
compel many of them to take the former alternative.   For it will very soon be found that
there is little or no available money to be got
hold of, and, as a consequence, few buyers of
securities to be had. Private people will in
fact want to sell as well as banks, in order to
get cash for trade purposes. Depositors may
then also begin to take alarm, and by asking
for their cash force some banks to close their
doors ; the reserve of the Bank of England
will become depleted, and we shall find ourselves, as usual, issuing a practically incon-

vertible paper currency in order to allay public apprehension.

At the same time, I am bound to confess that I think the majority of the English joint-stock banks will ride through the storm, at considerable cost to their shareholders perhaps, but still they will ride it through. Some of them are very strong, in spite of the bad times, and would be perfectly solvent even if compelled to shut their doors for a time; others are solvent though not strong; and nearly all of any consequence are backed by a proprietary capable in time of making losses good. What is really to be dreaded in present circumstances is the condition of the private banks, about which we know absolutely nothing with any degree of certainty, and of which, therefore, I have not spoken. We may safely conclude, however, that they have been in no way exempt from the errors and temptations of their joint-stock neighbours, and we can at least be sure that in many cases they are not backed as joint-stock banks are, by a wealthy proprietary. There is, indeed, too much reason to believe that not a few of them are so poor as to be mere skeletons, and the failure of one large old private bank would be something more alarming, and fraught with deeper mischief, than almost anything else that could happen. I therefore think that the next financial crisis in this country will produce a radical change in the condition of all private banks, and perhaps seal the fate of many among them.

It will also, I hope, cause the introduction of several reforms which are very much needed in joint-stock banking. It should stop, for example, the present foolish race after preposterously high dividends, and introduce greater frequency, uniformity, and fulness in the published balance-sheets. If the crisis at the same time reads the community a sharp lesson in regard to the practices which now prevail of using bank balances as a medium for gambling, and teaches bankers to be less ready to lock up capital which should be strictly 'floating' in securities which, when the time comes, refuse to ' float,' the ultimate outcome must be good for the commercial stability of the country.

CHAPTER II.

THE banking crisis through which the country
has been passing since October last, has fully
justified the anticipations of the article forming
the previous chapter. Although it arose in a
quarter outside the range of that article, the
symptoms of distress manifested by many English banks, and the losses they have sustained,
sufficiently prove that their condition was such
as I had described. People are now hoping
that the worst of the crisis is past. Its effects
are still visible, but the banks have stood
the severe strain put upon them so well that
there is fair ground for this hope. All the
hidden rottenness may not be brought to light,
but the worst of it perhaps has been ; and at
anyrate the banks deserve the utmost credit for
the manner in which their difficulties have been
so far met. Some of them have paid away
millions of money to depositors, and are to-
day fully able to meet the demand for millions
more. In a sense some of them may be said to

be stronger now than they were before pressure on their resources began. Their liabilities are less, and therefore more wieldy. They have consequently less temptation to launch into bad business.

All this is true; and yet there are many points connected with our modern system of banking which demand the most serious consideration from the country at large and from the Legislature. We cannot afford to sit down and say 'all is well,' merely because the strain has so far been successfully borne. The calamities of the City of Glasgow Bank failure and of subsequent bank suspensions have been of too painful and disastrous a character to permit us to neglect the warnings or disregard the lessons they are calculated to teach. We must find out what these failures portend, and whether we can safely regard the features disclosed by them as something apart from the ordinary banking business of the country. Did they arise out of our banking habits by a natural process of growth and development, or are we to regard them as altogether of the nature of diseased excrescences? These are questions of the highest moment, and their answer demands at our hands a further analysis of some of the leading characteristics of English banking. If we see that these are from their nature likely

to produce unsoundness, then we must endeavour to find out how to reform them.

At the very threshold of the inquiry we are
in danger of being led astray by the intensity
of the feelings to which the disasters of the
past few months have given rise. The
circumstances and character of the City of
Glasgow Bank suspension are in a measure
burned in on the popular mind. It was a calamity so unlooked for, so huge and disastrous,
that it riveted men's gaze and made their hearts
stand still, and we shall all remember it to our
dying day as a landmark in the history of our
generation. There is, therefore, in one sense,
small necessity for me to enter into details
about this failure, and yet the very magnitude
of it has tended to obscure some of its most
notable features. We have been stunned and
horrified at the same time, and on recovering
senses and breath, poured out wrath and condemnation upon the men who caused the misery
and ruin, tacitly assuming that the causes which
produced such a disaster could exist only in the
diabolical machinations of those instrumental in
bringing it about. Everybody joined in cen-
suring the directors and managers, but in doing
so forgot that there might be more important
things to be attended to than even their punishment. By all means let these men be con-

demned, for they are worthy to be held up as a warning to evil-doers for all time, but in consigning them to their own place, let us not forget to ask, How was it possible for such frauds as those of the City of Glasgow Bank to be committed ? That is the all-important question, and we must look at the history and surroundings of the bank in order to find an answer to it. Nay, we must go beyond that even, and look at the developments of what are called banking customs in all directions before we can get at the bottom of the matter. There have been other bank failures since that of the City of Glasgow, and under quite distinct conditions. Though less disastrous, because of smaller dimensions, these failures all tend to indicate that something is wrong in the 'system.' What is that something ? Is it one thing or many things ? If our banking habits and customs are deficient in safeguards or radically bad in any degree, we must mend them. Going on in the old way, after relieving the mind of a few maledictions on the heads of those who have fallen, will only lead to further mischief if things are wrong at the heart. Let us examine then the circumstances of the City of Glasgow Bank collapse, and one or two others, with a view to discover if reforms are needed, and what they must be.

One of the things most commonly heard

about the City of Glasgow Bank failure was
that it was due to the bank having departed
from the true system of Scotch banking, and
Scotch people in particular are never tired of in-
sisting upon this departure as the main cause of
the mischief.   In one sense they are right.   Old-
fashioned Scotch banking is a very peculiar and
very praiseworthy outcome of Scotch enterprise and thrift, and confined to Scotland, is
perhaps one of the safest kinds of banking in
existence.   But it has long ago ceased to be so
confined.   A majority of the existing Scotch
banks have overrun their borders and opened
offices in London, where they compete for
business with the banks that formerly were
their agents, and long before that was done
they had become inextricably mixed up with
the extensive colonial and foreign business of
the country.   This was inevitable, for Scotch-
men wander everywhere, and rise to commercial eminence everywhere.   Glasgow, too, has
become a mighty city, with trade ramifications extending to nearly every land under the
sun ; and as the business of Glasgow was done
by Scotch banks, their foreign connection could
not fail to become extensive.   Naturally, the
banks, in thus extending their business, continued to work on the old familiar lines which
had been found sufficient within Scotland.   It

was proudly asserted that no Scotch bank which
properly attended to its own peculiar business in
its peculiar Scotch way ever had failed, and the
stoppage of the Western Bank in 1857 was used
as an illustration in support of this assertion.
That bank, it was said, failed because it had
stepped out of its proper sphere, and by giving
large credits in New York and elsewhere, involved itself in foreign business over which it
had no control. Nothing could be more satisfactory or conclusive ; but then, we ask, what is
there in the Scotch system of banking to prevent the repetition of this offence ? And when
we look closely at that system, we find, to our
amazement, that there is nothing at all. On the
contrary, it distinctly fosters the kind of business which brought both the Western Bank and
the City of Glasgow Bank to ruin. Take the
balance-sheet of almost any Scotch bank that
you please, and, meagre as it always is, you will
find on the asset side, wrapped up with other
items of account, the word 'credits,' or the
phrase 'advances on cash and credit accounts,'
and if you ask what this means, you will discover that a large part of the business of Scotland is carried on by means of advances obtained
from the banks, with or without security. By
means of money thus obtained, generally on
personal security, or what amounts to the same

thing, on bonds, bills, or other 'cautionary' documents signed by third parties, men begin business in all walks of life, take shops, open factories, and work farms. The mere commercial bill-discounting of the Scotch banks thus comes to form a comparatively small portion of their business, and reduced to their essence they are to a large extent mortgage institutions, lending money at long dates, which they borrow from depositors under, as a rule, a contract to repay at fourteen days' notice.* Within Scot-

* A singular and most instructive light is thrown upon Scotch banking pure and simple, by the detailed balance-sheet recently presented to the shareholders of the Caledonian Banking Company. This respectable little bank became involved in the City of Glasgow Bank failure, through being registered as a holder of four of its shares, and the ruthless liquidators of that bank, in their determined pursuit of ' 20s. in the £, with interest till date of payment,' insisted, it is said, on pulling it down. Its stoppage revealed the strange fact that the bank was both sound and insolvent. That is to say its advances on cash credits and current account were so heavy that by no possibility could the bank have paid 20s. in the £ at the date of its suspension. At the head office in Inverness the cash credits and current account advances largely exceeded the total deposits, and at nearly all the branches these over-drafts, of various kinds, were very heavy. There were also many bills discounted overdue, and in short the whole statement is so curious that I have printed it in an appendix. If the reader will turn to the figures there given he will see, for example, that the cash credits and overdrawn accounts in Inverness exceed the total deposits and current account balances held there by £200,000. Practically speaking the Caledonian Bank was, there can be no doubt, insolvent at the date of its suspension, and yet in another sense it was sound enough. Misfortune overtook it at a bad time. Its customers had been struggling for years against the effects of bad harvests and low prices, and in their struggles they had

land, as I have said, this kind of business is probably as safe as banking can be, its principal weak spot being the liability to repay money immediately which may be practically lent for an indefinite period, or at least for months. So long, however, as the 'credits' given to struggling farmers and trades-people are confined to small amounts, and well distributed, the system works, on the whole, safely enough. But extend the system to the large operations of firms engaged in foreign trade, give to these huge open credits, *i.e.*, liberty to draw upon the bank for large sums of money, for the lending of which it has little security, or no security at all, and we are at once face to face with a momentous peril. The system which worked well in a small compass, slides easily into a position which makes it the vehicle for the most stupendous frauds. Scotch banks under it may spread their branches all over the country, not to act

been driven more and more back upon the bank for help. So long as the bank was distributing this help all over its districts in small sums to individual borrowers, it was doing a valuable work, and one that has always been a very honourable feature of Scotch banking. It could in ordinary circumstances only fail through doing such work when the community itself failed. A few years of good harvests coming after the bad time would have brought back much of its money, overdue bills would have been paid, overdrafts cleared off, and the whole situation made more easy. As it happened, the bank was pulled up just at the very worst time, and its weaknesses disclosed when they could least bear inspection. Hence its practical insolvency.

as supports to local enterprise, but as suckers
which draw in to the central office the means
for supporting far-reaching speculations.

A point like this must not be forgotten in
discussing the meaning of the City of Glasgow
Bank fraudulent collapse.   A *résumé* of the
principal features of its history will suffice to
prove at once that the collapse was eventually
brought about, not by a departure from, but
by an undue expansion of the system of business which is a peculiar feature of Scotch banking, and to a large extent of English provincial banking also.   If I might so phrase it,
the managers of the City of Glasgow Bank
diverged into fraud by following the tra-
ditional banking system of the country too
foolishly and too far.   At the outset nothing
was probably further from their thoughts than
crime.   This bank was never a strong one,
and after its temporary stoppage in 1857, was
for a long time distrusted.   As bankers would
say, it was in 'poor credit.'   It, however, did a
large business in Glasgow, and the usual exi-
gencies of that business compelled it to follow
the example of its neighbours, and give free
accommodation to its customers.   This accommodation consisted largely in granting 'cash
credits' to certain firms, and after a time these
unsecured advances landed the bank in heavy

losses. Being a weak bank, its managers were afraid to face these losses. The revelation of them might have led to its suspension, and so it was thought better to try and 'nurse' the bad accounts and insolvent firms, trusting to better times for recovery of the loss. You may call such a decision mad or unprincipled if you like, but it is what all Scotch and other bankers are more or less in the habit of doing every day of their lives. In the case of the City of Glasgow Bank affairs did not mend. On the contrary, they went as usual from bad to worse, and when the disastrous fall in silver took place after the close of the Franco-Prussian war, the losses of the firms in the Eastern trade, which the bank was supporting, became stupendous. Hope died away in the breasts of those responsible for these losses, and in the end they lost their heads, grew reckless, criminal, desperate, and plunged headlong into this wild speculation and that in the mad endeavour to stave off inevitable ruin. Land in Australia and New Zealand was bought with the bank's money, at prices far beyond its realisable value ; railways in the United States whose paper would not float there or anywhere else, found refuge and money in the City of Glasgow Bank, rotten firms and unscrupulous adventurers grew to be such tyrants over it in its helplessness, that

they had what cash from it they wanted for
the asking, and the bare hint of stoppage
on the part of any one of them seems to have
paralysed the directors with terror.   Thus when
the end came, the deficiency of the bank was
found to be about £6,800,000, including the
paid-up capital and reserve.   It was the most
stupendous banking collapse that the world had
ever seen, and naturally men cried out that it
was due to utter rascality, and to the defiance of
all sound banking customs.   No doubt it was
so, but I repeat, it began through adherence to
the Scotch system of banking, and its outward
conformity to that system to the very last,
served to hide its utter rottenness from all
its neighbours.   On to that system had been
tacked the modern practice of accepting bills.
The bank, that is to say, suffered the people
who were sucking it dry to draw upon it bills,
which it accepted against credits opened in
its books, and then, when the bills became
due, paid them either with money out of its
till—money drawn from its country depositors,
or if the market would take them, with money
obtained on fresh batches of bills.   As the game
grew desperate, and the weight of these acceptances became too much for the London market,
the bank had to discount some of them itself
through third parties.   Thus losses accumulated

on every hand, and each year saw a larger and
larger portion of the assets of the bank, of its
trusting customers' money, irretrievably gone.
But the whole swindle was done more or less
in conformity with banking practices, Scotch
and English, to the very last, and it unquestionably began in what would be considered a
legitimate application of these practices. The
very fact that all its neighbours remained to
the last ignorant of the danger at their doors,
and that at the last the London market was
'caught' with between two and three millions
sterling of the City of Glasgow Bank's finance
paper, is enough to demonstrate the absurdity of
the plea that this failure arose out of a departure
from banking usages. It was due to an undue
extension of these usages, and to nothing else.

Had the business of the City of Glasgow
Bank been diverging altogether from the
wonted banking habits of the community,
would it have been possible for the divergence
to remain long unknown? If it would, we are reduced to the painful necessity of concluding that
its neighbours were all fools. As we cannot
accept that conclusion, we are driven to the
alternative one, that the City of Glasgow Bank
was really making no departure from the customs of its neighbours. It granted credits as
they did, and allowed its debtors to draw

against these credits just as they did. Wise
after the event, bankers have set up the usual
chorus, 'We all knew,' and call to the recollec-
tion of their friends the fact that 'they had
always said the City of Glasgow Bank had too
many acceptances afloat.' Of course they
said that, but what does that prove? Just
nothing at all, for the same thing has been said
time out of mind about half-a-dozen other
banks that I could name, whose business goes
on and seems to flourish to this day.

There is no getting out of the dilemma then.
The City of Glasgow Bank merely did as its
neighbours do, with only this difference, that
being weak it suffered a few firms, and ultimately a group of gamblers, to get so deep in
its debt, that it became their abject though
secret slave. Its managers made away with
other people's money, and hid the theft for
years, because they were slaves; but they became slaves by doing in the first instance just
as their neighbours did, and to the last they
stole in proper banking form. The conclusion
therefore to which we are driven, is that the
Scotch banking system is capable of being easily
'developed' into a medium for fraud, now that
the field of its operations has become extended
on every side. It is a system, in short, which,
when aided by 'acceptances,' may well be

worked in a manner that makes fraud probable, for it is one which draws the banks into dangerous risks almost in spite of themselves.

Let us now see how it stands with failed English banks. We have had only one large joint-stock bank failure in England—that of the West of England and South Wales District Bank, and the conditions of English banking are naturally much more varied than those of Scotch banking. We have London banks and provincial banks, and joint-stock and private banks, all governed by traditions and customs more or less varied. There are also Indian and Colonial banks, whose chief offices are in London, and the nature of whose business induces peculiar habits. All these we shall presently subject to more or less examination ; but in the meantime this West of England Bank failure may be cited as offering a remarkable confirmation of the soundness of the conclusions arrived at in the preceding chapter. It has failed because it was drawn into heavy advances on securities once thought to be good, but now unrealisable except at a serious loss. Like the City of Glasgow Bank, its failure involves calls on the shareholders, though to a smaller amount. For years the balance-sheets of the bank must have been false, and its profits more or less illusory. Yet the directors have not been arrested, nor

accused of fraud. Why is this distinction
drawn? For a very simple reason. The West
of England Bank directors made no false entries
in their balance - sheets or books. All the
figures they put down represented some equivalent reality. They had lent so many hundreds
of thousands to Booker & Co., or to the Ply-
mouth & Aberdare Co., and they held something
against these advances as security. All that they
did was to ignore the fall in the value of this
supposed security. It was just as if by some
mysterious power bags once filled with gold had
become stuffed with chaff, but notwithstanding this disastrous change, still figured in the
books as so many bags of gold. The directors
'hoped,' and were victims of a too sanguine
disposition, to such an extent that, when the
end came, the bank was found a loser by
nearly £1,300,000. Nothing wrong was done
by anybody, nor did the bank managers think
that they had gone beyond banking customs in
their dealings.

Attentively considered, therefore, this failure illustrates what I take to be one peculiar
danger of English provincial banking. Provincial banks have acquired the habit of lending
to firms upon their fixed property. Mill-
owners obtain loans on the security of their
mills, coal-owners on the security of their

mines and iron-works on the security of their plant. This is nominally a different kind of lending from the Scotch 'cash-credit' system, inasmuch as the bank takes what is called 'security' for the loans; but in its results it is, perhaps, fully more dangerous; because directly the security becomes depreciated, the lending bank stands in danger of being saddled with larger losses than the Scotch credit system, unaided by acceptances, usually entails. It cannot realise and get its money back any more than the 'open credit' giving bank, because depreciation means in all such cases the practical unsaleability of the 'security,' except at a sacrifice which few bankers, when left to themselves, have the courage to face. The alternative of 'nursing' is, therefore, here again usually resorted to, the loss is not written off, and in the end the bank may become insolvent. A loan upon inconvertible security or real estate is thus a most dangerous asset for a bank, and, above all, a deposit bank, to touch with money which it may be called upon to refund at any moment; and the fact that English provincial banks deal more or less largely in these loans, is one of the gravest possible significance at the present time. A further depreciation of real property, of mines and manufactories, may yet come

upon us before trade revives, and beyond
question that cannot take place without involving several banks still considered solvent
in heavy losses and possibly in bankruptcy.

Here again, then, the bank failure has not
been due to exceptional or extraordinary
causes, but to such as are common to many
banks. Custom has sanctioned business of
the kind done by the West of England Bank
to a much greater extent than sound banking
theories would permit ; and we owe it to the
prudence of individual managers, and to that
alone, if one bank is found standing clear of
risks such as bring its neighbours to the
ground. Wherever the balance - sheets examined in the preceding chapter give indications of the nature of the business done,
they show that this development of banking
has been on the increase—this and the habit
of giving credit to distressed customers ; but as
the dangers thus arising to banks have been
already sufficiently dwelt upon, I shall not
enlarge further upon them here. Before pro-
ceeding, however, to discuss other peculiarities
of banking, or the legal and other checks and
remedies which they may demand, I should
like to draw the reader's attention for a moment
to the failure of a private bank in Rochdale.
In one sense there was nothing very remark-

able in this failure, or at all events nothing
typical. Messrs. Fenton, the hereditary partners of this bank, had taken a stockbroker
into partnership, and this stockbroker had
gradually drawn the funds of the bank in to
the vortex of certain speculations in which
he was engaged, so that when the owners of
these funds came and demanded them they
were not forthcoming. This is a very simple,
but let us hope, a very exceptional kind of
complication. Very few persons have sufficient control of a bank to lock up nine-tenths
of its funds in their own operations. And
yet, exceptional though it might be, we fear it
was so only from its magnitude, not from its
nature. At every turn we see evidence of
the fact that in their own minds none of the
people instrumental in bringing these various
banks to ruin have felt, or feel now, that
they are morally guilty. They have been the
victims of adverse fortune. A little longer
time, a lucky chance or two, and they would
have pulled out of their difficulties all right.
This peculiar attitude of mind is one of the
most alarming symptoms of our time ; and it
is this which gives significance to the failure
of Messrs. Fenton & Son's bank. There may
be no more Jonathan Nields in the country,
so far as extent and boldness of operations are

concerned ; but there are a great many bankers
who, like him, see nothing wrong in similar
operations, and who when occasion offers
imitate them to the best of their power. Apart
from the extraordinary laxity which permitted
the manager of a bank to direct to his own
purposes, without let or hindrance, nearly the
whole of the bank's assets, there was nothing
in Mr. Nield's proceedings out of the ordinary.
We may, in short, take the failure of this
private bank as an illustration of a wide-spread
custom which sanctions the locking up of large
amounts of banking capital in unrealisable
stock-broking securities. Mr. Nield lent the
money to himself ; and other bankers, for the
most part, lend it to third parties. That is the
sole difference.

The custom of taking 'large lines' in stocks
is by no means so uncommon as many people
suppose, and it is one of the most dangerous
customs of the day. A bank may go on for
years prosperously lending to stockbrokers,
thereby aiding these to maintain stocks at fictitious values, and lose very little money. Yet
even that business has peculiarly heavy risks
in a time of difficulty, because should the
stockbrokers fail to find the money when
wanted, as they probably would, the bank
would be left with an unrealisable security.

That risk, however, is much smaller than the risk involved in out - and - out purchases of depreciated or second-class securities, or the kindred risk of large advances to Governments, syndicates of financiers, and the like, or on the 'security' of loans, or of bonds, or shares, to be issued at a future day. It is this latter kind of business which the Rochdale failure exemplifies, and many besides Mr. Jonathan Nield, of Rochdale, deeply commit themselves to it. Nothing could be more utterly foreign to the spirit and purpose of all banking as understood in this country. The most essential feature of that banking, it cannot be too often reiterated, is the approximate ready convertibility of all banking assets. Our banks all live and work on the assumed condition of being able to pay every deposit and other creditor in full, when called upon to do so ; and that condition imperatively demands that banks shall not lock up the money entrusted to them where it cannot be found when wanted. In actual business practice this is, of course, an impossible condition taken in its absolute sense, and therefore actual banking credit rests on a well-understood compromise. A kind of un-defined law of averages prevails, whose dictates are, that in order to be practically safe a bank must carefully subdivide its risks. If it is the

custom, as in Scotland and provincial England,
to give cash credits or liberty to overdraw, the
limit should be a narrow one, and the security,
personal or other, the best that can be obtainable. Also in lending to firms on the security of
deeds or bonds, the loans should be small in all
instances, so that the risks of the bank may be
divided to an extent which practically identifies
it with the wellbeing of the community. And
in stock-jobbing transactions, distribution and
subdivision of risks are as essential to sound
banking as in any other, while such transactions as advancing to loan mongers on un-
issued bonds of railways, Governments, muni-
cipalities, and the like, are in no sense bankers'
business at all.

Here, then, are at least three distinct 'banking
dangers,' which stand out clearly defined amid
the wrecks of the past six months. Every bank
failure of consequence, from the City of Glasgow
collapse downwards, has been due primarily
to a vice or vicious tendency inherent in the
banking customs of the country. There has
been a too free use of banking credit in some
given direction where banking credit is cus-
tomarily granted, and the money lent has been
lost. That is the sum of the matter. Therefore it is that these bank failures are warnings,
not mere phenomena to shake the head over

and pass by. They point to dangers that lie deep in the very heart of our banking system, and we must find means to guard against these dangers at all hazards in the future, lest a worse fate overtake us. What has happened may happen again, and indeed must happen, if we do not mend our ways in time.

CHAPTER III.

To be in strict sequence, I ought perhaps to examine, first of all, that peculiarly modern banking currency known as 'bank acceptances.' The City of Glasgow Bank managed to postpone the day of its collapse by means of these acceptances, and by means of them also the crash was all the more stupendous when it did come. This feature of banking has, however, so many ramifications, and is so much an outgrowth of banking habits prevalent beyond the reach of English law, strictly speaking, that I think it best to defer an examination of it until the to us more vitally important subject of banking law reforms has been disposed of. If the recent bank failures are due to dangers lying inherent in the banking customs of the country, the most important question for us is how to moderate these dangers. It is a question which we dare not let lie, without a practical answer ; and it must not be a mere 'put off' answer, either. A gulf of bottomless commercial perdition has been opened for a moment, as it were, beneath our feet; we have had a glimpse of the possible ruin that might overtake us all, of dangers threatening the very existence of England as a leader among commercial nations, and we cannot afford to disregard the warning thus given. If we had reason to suspect that these dangers are hidden in the very core of our modern banking habits, part of their hitherto masterful vitality, we must be prepared almost to revolutionise these habits, in order to get rid of them. To sit down now and say 'all is well' because there is a respite, because the storm has lulled for a time, because a new cycle of speculation, with its manifold chances of gain, may possibly be opening before us, would be more than folly. The bank failures that the country has suffered from warn us that we must not sit still. Smooth speeches will not do, there must be action. Not only must banking credit cease to be synonymous with systematic deception, as it too generally is now, but the very possibility of the terms becoming synonymous must, at all hazards, be removed. In one word, if we would save the country from many more City of Glasgow Bank failures, we must reform our banking customs, by bringing them within the scope of the law.

When we directly approach the subject of reform in this direction, the startling fact confronts us that our much belauded banking institutions exist in a state of chaos. There is literally and truly no well-defined banking law in the country, still less any well defined-banking habits. Outside the single point of the note circulation, the banks are left free to follow their own devices. In no other civilised or semi-civilised country does such a state of things exist as this discloses. We are therefore bewildered at the outset by the variety of forms and conditions of banking that we see around us, and the task of reducing them to something like order is enough to make any man despair. But into order they must be brought, and if reformers do not ask too much at once, good progress may be made, hopeless though the task at first sight appears. One can do no more here than indicate the main lines on which banking affairs ought to run.

Putting aside for the time being the private banks of the country, and dealing only with joint-stock institutions, we find, at the outset, a distinction which is of very great importance. Joint-stock banks may be constituted either on the 'limited' or the 'unlimited' liability principle, and until the recent failures took place, the latter was on the whole the form of

constitution most in favour, for the very
sufficient reason that it was thought by the
shareholders more conducive to profit, and by
the depositors, more likely to give safety. It
is the only form with which we need at present
concern ourselves. Under unlimited liability,
the shareholders of a bank are jointly and seve-
rally liable for its debts to the uttermost farthing they possess ; and amongst shareholders in
Scotland, under the ruling of a Scotch appeal
case—Lumsden *v.* Buchanan, are included trustees. The unheard of deficit of the City of
Glasgow Bank has brought home to the shareholders and trustees interested therein what a
liability of this kind may come to mean. Already a call of £500 per share has been made
upon that portion of the capital of the bank
in private hands, and hundreds of families have
been ruined thereby. But that is only the
beginning of the misery. Call upon call will
follow, until every individual connected with
the bank may be utterly ruined, and not these
alone. The shareholders of the Caledonian
Bank, which has been pulled down by the mere
prospect of what it might have ultimately to pay
as the registered owner of four shares in the
Glasgow Bank, may also be all ruined before
the ideal 20s. and interest is realised. So
intense is the suffering and misery which the

failure has produced, that business in Scotland
has become paralysed. The Scotch have lost
their heads in the midst of the horrors of the
disaster, and grave, responsible men amongst
them have gone so far as to try to break or defy
the law of the land in a despairing endeavour to
bring relief to the distressed shareholders. Such
is the practical meaning of unlimited liability.

Naturally a calamity such as this has opened
the eyes of the community to the dangers
which lurk beneath the fair, prosperous appear-
ances of unlimited joint-stock banking. People
rushed to sell their shares, not in Scotch banks
alone, but in English also, and bank directors,
alarmed both at the fall and at the prospect of
a deterioration in the quality of the names on
their shareholders' registers, have set up a common cry for some change whereby the liability
of all bank shareholders may be limited and
defined. The matter has gone so far, that if
the bankers can but agree on what they want,
the Chancellor of the Exchequer is said to be
ready to submit a bill to Parliament during the
ensuing session. What the bankers may decide
on is not yet certain ; but from what has tran-
spired about their desires, I am disposed to think
that they seek a measure which those people
interested in unlimited joint-stock banks, either
as depositors, or as ordinary customers pos-

sessed of a balance at their credit, ought to
oppose. For when we look closely at the
position of unlimited banks, we find that they
cannot change that position without changing
many things not contemplated by the uneasy
directors or frightened shareholders. Round
this question there lies, in fact, others far more
vital, which must be satisfactorily settled before
it can be even looked at. It is a remarkable
fact, in view of the present clamour for limitation of liability, that until last October it was
the pride and ambition of bank managers and
directors to make their institutions unlimited.
The 'limited liability banks' were looked down
upon as institutions of a petty kind, dwarfed
by the very restrictions now so much belauded,
and incapable of more than a feeble existence.
The higher feats of banking were not for
them, and the reason of this was very plain.
Unlimited banks had an enormous advantage
over their competitors in the struggle for deposits. A depositor would be much more
likely to trust his money with a bank whose
shareholders he knew must yield up to him
the uttermost farthing that they possessed, in
making good losses should the bank fail, than
with a bank whose shareholders were liable
only to the amount uncalled on their shares.
Therefore banks on all hands took advantage of

the law, and registered themselves as 'unlimited,' and by this means have drawn to
themselves enormous amounts of money.
There are three banks whose head offices
are in London, the aggregate liabilities of
which to depositors and on current account
balances amount at the present time to nearly
£70,000,000, and they are all unlimited. Now
the question which forces itself upon the attention from the point of view of the owners of
all that money is this : ought these banks to
be permitted to limit the liability of their
shareholders in a manner that might prevent
repayment in full of all their liabilities, should
they from any cause go the way of the City of
Glasgow Bank ? In other words, would not
limitation of liability in these cases, if granted
now, imply a grave breach of contract if it
were effective limitation as regards its shareholders ? To my mind there can be but one
answer to such a question. The unlimited
banks cannot be allowed to contract themselves
out of the obligations which they have deliberately incurred, unless prepared at the same
time to grant safeguards in another direction
of sufficient stringency to afford more protection to the public. In the race after the money
of depositors, banks chose to become 'unlimited,' and thereby obtained enormous sums.

They ought not to be permitted now to turn
round in a fright and say, 'We shall only pay
you 10s. in the pound, or 5s. in the pound,
if the worst come to the worst.' That is
practically what they do say by their present
clamour for power to limit their liability on
shares ; and if they are to have their way, the
public must say, 'Very well, then limit your
liability ; but give us, in the first place, the
right to look after you, so that you may be
compelled to stop payment should your losses
ever approach the line fixed by the limitation
you may make.' A stipulation of this kind is
absolutely necessary as preliminary to any concession, when we consider such a fact as this,
for example, that a limitation of the liability
on shares of a bank like the London and
Westminster to £500 per share, would not half
cover its present reduced indebtedness to depositors and customers.

This consideration, therefore, brings us at
once to the main point at issue between banks
and the public at the present time. In nothing
is the freedom, I may say the lawlessness, of our
banking institutions more visible than in the total
disregard which their managers have uniformly
shown towards both shareholders and depositors in the matter of information about their
affairs. You have had to take everything on

trust as regards your banker ; and blind faith is the one virtue which the shareholders and depositors have always had to exercise. This applies in a special sense to unlimited and private banks, but compared with what is done in other countries all our banks sin most grievously in this respect. The unlimited liability custom has here again unquestionably played a conspicuous part in sending men to sleep. Yet there is no system of banking which more imperatively demands thorough supervision than this, or than ours in all its ramifications. For one thing, the practice of giving interest on deposits has become so ingrained in our banking habits, affecting all kinds of banks—unlimited joint-stock, unlimited private, chartered, and limited—that it has been the means of swelling the total liabilties of the banks of the kingdom on interest-bearing deposits alone to probably about £300,000,000. The gross liability of all the banks on deposit and current accounts is not much if at all short of £600,000,000. Now, what are depositors but sleeping partners in the business ? They are in a sense bankers just as shareholders are bankers, since both parties entrust their money to certain men with a view to profit. The essential difference is that in the case of joint-stock banks the shareholders contract to hold the depositors indemnified in the

event of loss. Take away this indemnification
to any extent and the depositors become almost
as deeply interested in the good management
of the bank as the shareholders. On this
narrow ground alone, therefore, it is imperative
that all banks taking deposits should be compelled to give information about their affairs of
a kind hitherto withheld. Shareholders and depositors alike have claims on managers of joint-
stock banks which it has been the practice to
ignore, and not these alone. The broad ground
of general public interests demands that all
banks, joint-stock and private, be compelled to
render periodical accounts setting forth their
position, and that these accounts should be
certified by some independent authority. So
much is this the case, that reform in this direction
is far more essential to safety and good banking
than limited liability. Those who clamour for
that, lead themselves and others astray, and
follow a mere shadow. In one sense all banks
limit their liability most effectually by their constitution. Had the City of Glasgow Bank, for
example, been subjected to such supervision as
would have revealed its losses in 1870 or in 1868,
it would have been compelled by its memoran-
dum of copartnery to stop payment, and the
shareholders would have lost nothing but a portion of the value of the shares they held, with the

premiums thereon.   In like manner, the Chairman of the London Joint-Stock Bank stated
the other day at the half-yearly meeting, that if
the reserve fund and one-fourth of the paid-up
capital was lost, the bank must, by the law of its
being, be wound up.   What do these revelations
point to if not to this—that banks in order to
be safe want outside supervision far more than
arbitrary limitation of shareholders' liability ?
Events have proved abundantly that the managers and directors of banks cannot themselves
be trusted to exercise this supervision.   They refuse to admit losses which stare them in the face.
They go on and on, hoping against hope, till the
ruin becomes too horrible for the ruined to realise,
and stare in blank astonishment when it breaks
upon their heads, just as if they knew no cause
for it.   And now that they find shareholders
alarmed, deposits withdrawn, and general distrust prevailing, they cry 'limit our liability.'
The true answer to that cry is—make arrangements to give effect to the limitations you already possess.   Take a broad common-sense
view of your position, and, if you have nothing to
hide, be ready to prove that you have nothing.

In my view of the matter, looking at the
extraordinary examples of folly and self-decep-
tion which the City of Glasgow Bank has given
us, which other failures display every day of our

lives, there are two practical banking reforms absolutely wanted, and two only, so far as the law of the land goes. The one is the audit of bank accounts by independent authorities outside the directorate or the copartnery, and the other is the periodical publication of banking balance-sheets properly certified by the auditors. The latter reform all the chairmen who have spoken at recent meetings have professed great willingness to submit to, but they kick at the former, and with equal unanimity. Yet the latter without the former is of no value. It would not be possible to frame a balance-sheet which could not be made a vehicle of fraud and deception, if the compilers of it so chose, and an audit to establish the authenticity of the balance-sheets of all banks is consequently essential to any banking reform worth the name. Certainly, without submitting to both these conditions, no unlimited bank should be permitted to become 'limited.' A glaring wrong will be done to the community if they are in this respect let off without a satisfactory concession.

Strong objections have, however, been made to the 'audit' of bank accounts by the mouthpieces and authorities of all unlimited banks. Limited banks already submit to a kind of audit, and have therefore nothing to say.

These objections when scrutinised do not seem
of a very solid kind, and may be said to resolve
themselves into these two : — (1) an audit is
unnecessary, and (2) an effective audit is impracticable. It is unnecessary, say the bank
chairmen, 'because we audit the accounts ourselves.' Sir John Rose drew a remarkable picture of the thoroughness of this 'audit' at the
London and Westminster meeting in January
last. According to his statement, the bank
appears to be managed by committees of
directors, who hedge round their nominal
official manager with safeguards and restrictions till, so far as we can see, his work might
be as well done by an ordinary ledger clerk.
These committees supervise everything, and a
'continuous audit' thus goes on, which is declared to be far more satisfactory than any em-
pirical hasty outside audit could even be. That
phrase, a 'continuous audit,' was marvellously
adroit, and took the public fancy so much that
we find it repeated on every hand as a complete reply to all objectors. This being so, it
may seem unkind to quarrel with it, and yet
the facts compel me to set it and the whole
of this special plea down as practical nonsense.
I cannot shut my eyes to the history of the
London and Westminster Bank for the past
five years, and the singular commentary which

that history is on this wonderful system of audit. In spite of these elaborate directorial checks, and this continuous systematic scrutiny of the bank's affairs, there has hardly been a gigantic commercial failure since 1874 in which the London and Westminster has not been more or less deeply involved. How are we to reconcile the benefits of the elaborate provisions described by Sir John Rose with a fact like that? If such complete supervision did not prevent the bank from having to write £500,000 off its reserve to help to cover the losses incurred in the Collie and Aberdare failures, if it did not prevent the bank from having £114,000 of City of Glasgow Bank acceptances in hand on its own account at the date of the failure, besides the large amounts held on account of bill-brokers of little or no means, with whom it does business, it is clearly of no avail as a safeguard to either shareholders or depositors.

These very City of Glasgow Bank acceptances afford a remarkable instance of the delusions to which bank managers and directors are subject when brought face to face with possibilities of losses. It is worth while pausing for a moment to see how this matter stands. The investigators' balance-sheet showed the City of Glasgow Bank to be owing £2,742,000 on ac-

ceptances at the date of its suspension, and there
was known to be upwards of £100,000 additional indebtedness floating about the market
in the shape of bills of the bank's insolvent
customers discounted without its acceptance.
Altogether, therefore, the paper of this bank
and its bankrupt customers amounted to nearly
£2,900,000 at the date of the bank's suspension. Of that paper a very small proportion
has been retired by third parties, not, I believe, £200,000 in all; so that at the very lowest
estimate there is more than £2,600,000 of it
still in the hands of the creditors of the bank.
Now it is a remarkable fact, that the total
amount acknowledged by the London banks
and discount houses in their half-yearly reports
is less than £800,000.* The Scotch banks

* The following are the amounts of the City of Glasgow
Bank acceptances acknowledged to be held by London banks
and discount houses :—

London and County Bank,*	{ £167,600, Glasgow Bank.
	57,334, other firms in con-
	nection therewith.
Alliance Bank, . . .	12,155
City Bank, ...	18,000
London and Westminster Bank,	114,000
Union of Australia,† . .	5,000
General Credit and Discount,.	47,437
National Discount, . . .	156,000
United Discount, . . .	219,000
	£796,526

* Of which £17,198 had, at the date when last half-year's report was made up, been
covered or cleared off.
† Of this total £3000 had been received at the date of the meeting, or January 13th.

are stated to hold in one way or other from £400,000 to £600,000, and, according to a list in my possession, have directly proved on the estates of the insolvent firms for about £340,000. Take their total interest at £600,000, and we have still, on the most favourable estimate, nearly £1,500,000 of the known amount of this paper unaccounted for. Where are the bills which represent this sum? A certain proportion of them is no doubt held by Colonial and Indian banks which have as yet made no statement, or by private bankers who make no report to the public at all; but from all one can learn, it seems improbable that so much as £400,000 is thus held; and there can be not the least doubt that for the most part the bills are in the possession of these very banks which say that their interest in the failure is only so much. The banks did not take these bills direct; they are merely pawned to them by the bill discounters who got them in the open market, and inasmuch as they bear these bill-discounters' endorsements, the banks say, 'That class of bill is not to be taken as a liability of ours; it is So-and-So's.' Yet 'So-and-So' cannot 'lift' these bills; and were the bank to fall short of full payment of them by 2s. 6d. in the pound, 'So-and-So' would probably fail and throw the loss on the

F

bank. Most of the private bill discounters
who took these bills to the banks are, in short,
mere go-betweens, used by the banks for lending their money—men with little or no capital,
who could do nothing to assist the bank in
meeting losses on this or any other pile of
accommodation paper. For all that, as I believe, the banks treat these men's names on the
bills as something solid between them and loss
on about, in round figures, £1,000,000 of City
of Glasgow Bank paper. They refuse to take
the bills which they are compelled to hold as
their own liability, and say, 'We have only so
much interest in this great disaster.' A more
remarkakle instance of the sanguine tempera-
ment of bankers it would not be possible to
find.

We must speak out plainly on this subject.
Bank directors and managers are not in the
nature of things to be trusted to audit their
own accounts, and it is monstrous that they
should make the claim to do so. They cannot
·help taking an over sanguine view of bad or
doubtful transactions ; they have the strongest
possible inducements to minimise losses, and
will always do so. How, to take but one
example, is the board of a bank which gives
loans to its own directors to be trusted to
assess the amount of losses which may be

incurred through these advances? Let the
story of the City of Glasgow Bank crime
furnish the answer. What was done by the
board there will be done elsewhere when
necessity urges.

'That may be all very true,' say others;
'we grant you that an audit is highly desirable,
but in the case of banks of the magnitude of
the Westminster, the London and County, or
the National Provincial, an outside audit is
entirely impracticable. It could not be done
by any accountant in existence within six
months at the very least.' If this be true, the
true answer to it is—then these banks are all
too big, for accounts that men cannot audit
other men cannot keep in order. But that the
assertion is true only in a relative sense is
proved by the mere fact, that banks as large as
the Westminister and London and County do
have an audit of a kind. The accounts of the
London and County profess to be audited each
half-year by a committee of shareholders, and
if these can do the work efficiently, why cannot
a professional auditor? I admit freely that if it
be the business of an auditor to overhaul all
the accounts of the bank, and to assess the
value of all its securities, he could not audit the
accounts of a bank like the London and County
or the National Provincial, with their numerous

branches, within twelve months. But that is not what I mean, nor what any sensible person means by a banking audit. What is really desired is not an inquisition into a bank's affairs, but a check on fraud, and for the purposes of such a check much less than this scrutiny is required.

The one absolutely essential thing is that the audit shall be independent, and in order to be so, it ought to be done by parties entirely outside the bank. It must also be a skilful audit, and that condition can only be met by the employment of professional auditors. Shareholders are as a rule practically useless for such a purpose; their interest is the same as that of the directors and managers, viz., to keep the credit of the bank good at all hazards.

In order to define more clearly the object and scope of what I venture to call true banking audit, suffer me to diverge here to the question of bank balance-sheets. They are at once the test and measure of efficient audit, and if we can settle on an intelligible basis the lines on which published bank balance-sheets ought to be framed, we shall go a great way towards defining the limits of bank audit. Some short time ago I drew up a form of bank balance-sheet, which, on its publication in a morning newspaper, was

the subject of a good deal of criticism. So far
that criticism was gratifying, in that, while ob-
jecting to minor details, the objectors never
went the length of saying—' You ask the
bankers for too much,' except on one point,
to which I shall presently refer. Profiting by
the suggestions and criticisms which this *pro
forma* balance-sheet drew forth, I have sought
to amend and improve its details, and now
submit it for the consideration of the reader
in a more complete form :—

BANK BALANCE-SHEET.

LIABILITIES.		ASSETS.	
To capital paid up,	£1,500,000	By cash in hand,	£400,000
To reserve fund,	500,000	By cash at Bank of England,	500,000
To notes in circulation,	350,000	By loans to bill-brokers, at call and at notice, not exceeding 14 days,	1,000,000
To deposits bearing interest,	3,200,000		
To current and other accounts, with credit balances,	7,700,000	By loans to stockbrokers, at call or till next S.E. account,	900,000
To cash borrowed on bills rediscounted,	1,000,000	By investments, viz.* :— Consols, India Government bonds, Colonial Government bonds, English railway debentures,	3,000,000
To acceptances as *per contra*,	500,000		
Against which are held as security—		By bills discounted, not yet due,	4,500,000
Cash, £50,000		By bills discounted, overdue,	100,000
Bills with documents attached, 400,000		By loans to customers for fixed periods on convertible securities (present value of securities exceeding £——),	1,500,000
Other securities at market value, exceeding 150,000		By loans to customers for fixed periods on mercantile security (nominal value of security £——),	1,000,000
Uncovered credits, 100,000		By overdue loans and loans on security, the value of which is unascertainable,	500,000
£700,000		By advances on personal security, or without security,	750,000
To balance brought down,	10,000	By acceptances as *per contra*,	500,000
To rebate do. do.,	20,000	By bank buildings, £350,000	
To gross profits for half-year,	220,000	Less value written off, 100,000	250,000
		By current expenses, interest due, etc.,	100,000
	£15,000,000		£15,000,000

* Only one or two examples of investment are given here, but the designations
and amounts of all ought to be completely exhibited.

PROFIT AND LOSS ACCOUNT.

Dr.			*Cr.*	
To rebate on bills at bank rate,	£25,000	By balance brought forward, . .	£10,000
To interest due to depositors,	35,000	By rebate do. do., . .	20,000
To bad debts written off, .	10,000	By gross profits as per balance-sheet,	220,000
To loss allowed on doubtful debts, ...	20,000		
To salaries of staff at head office, and branch rent, stamps, taxes, etc. . . .	52,000		
To directors' fees, . . .	3,000		
To addition to reserve, . .	20,000		
To dividend to shareholders, at the rate of 10 per cent. per annum, ...	75,000		
To balance carried forward, .	20,000		
	£250,000		£250,000

AUDITORS' CERTIFICATE.

We have examined the books of the bank with the vouchers, and found them correct. The entries in the above balance-sheet also correspond with the entries in the books. Further, we have ascertained the correctness of the items of cash and bills of exchange, and have inspected the investments and securities held by the bank, and find them to be in its possession as above stated. We also certify that no individual or corporate customer of the bank has advances to the extent of one-fifth of the paid-up capital, and that the allowances for bad and doubtful debts are in accordance with the actual amount of bad debts and doubtful accounts to be found in the books.

A careful study of the items of this balance-sheet will not, I am persuaded, discover that there is any material point in it upon which bankers ought not to be willing to give information. Our banking institutions, public and private, must recognise that the day for concealment is past. Banking business is no longer a fetish to be worshipped blindly. The confidence bred of intelligence must supersede the take-all-for-granted superstition. As a first step to this progress, it seems to me essential that all banks in the country, joint-stock and private, should be compelled to set forth twice a year some such balance-sheet as the model here given. There would be modifications, of course ; some banks have note

circulations, others none ; some give credits to
their customers without security, others do
not.   Many country banks rediscount their
bills with London brokers or bankers; few
London banks do so—they 'accept' instead,
and so on.   Colonial and Indian banks habitually take deposits at long dates, averaging, I
believe, from one to five years, and they might
be made to set forth the particulars of these
deposits ; but with such exceptions this balance-
sheet probably contains all that could fairly be
demanded of the banks.   Most of what is here
asked they would, I believe, be willing to con-
cede, with one important exception.   They are
most reluctant to be forced to set forth their
losses by bad and doubtful debts.   'It would
never do,' they one and all declare.   'Some
half-year we might make a big loss, and if we
could not hide it up we should bring shareholders and depositors about our ears.   Anything you like to ask but this.   This we cannot
give.'   That is the declaration, and it is what
the traditions of banking lead us to expect.
But there is no reason in the plea ; it is a
very bad one, however looked at, embracing,
as it does, everything that the City of Glasgow
or other fraudulent bank directors could urge
in justification of their conduct.   For all that,
bankers cling to it.   They dread the unknown

in this respect, accustomed as they are to conceal losses when made, to glose over bad debts, and generally to put as good a face as possible on ugly bits of business. That the daylight should be let in on this system may now be imperative, but the bankers none the less resent it. A more curious example than this plea of the strange vagaries to which modern commercial morality is subject could not be given.

It demonstrates, with greater force than any conceivable argument, the absolute need for an independent audit. A balance-sheet such as this would be entirely, or almost entirely, useless without such an audit; because it is impossible to make this or any other model balance-sheet an absolute preventive of deception. Banking safety, in short, does not lie in any prescribed form of published accounts, but in the steps taken to make the form a reality.

Now, it will be plain to any unprejudiced mind that the items of the above-given balance-sheet offer no obstacle to the practically effective audit of any bank, however large. The auditors are not, speaking generally, called upon to certify to anything beyond the correctness of the book entries. In a month's time such an audit as this balance-sheet demands could be carried through in the largest bank in the kingdom. the first few times that the work had to be done it might take longer, but once the system was in order, and the auditors had become familiar with the operations of the bank, their work would simplify itself and become practically easy enough. The auditors would check the various classes of bank books, count the cash, examine the investments, scrutinise the loan returns, and generally find out whether the entries on the debit and credit sides of the account balanced. Into the question of the value of this or that banking security it would be no part of their duty to go, except where losses had been incurred or were threatening. The audit would merely indicate the nature of each class of security—house property, stock, dock warrants, whatever it might be. I repeat that this could be done with the largest bank in the kingdom with no insurmountable difficulty.

Admitting all this, some bankers unwilling to surrender at discretion fall back on the further difficulty implied in the question, Who is to effect such an audit ? Some say the Government must do it ; others that the Government ought to have nothing to do with banking, for the simple reason that its interference might lead to more evil than it could cure. 'What, then, is to be the true means for securing a good audit ?' This is, perhaps, the most difficult

point of all ; but I do not even believe it to be
insurmountable.   It is only difficult, indeed,
because of the low standard of professional
morality which the existing bankruptcy law has
developed amongst professional accountants.
What is really wanted, therefore, is some means
of raising the prevailing standard of morals
amongst the members of this most useful and
valuable class of men.   And the Government,
although taking no part in audits, might indirectly help to do this by demanding substantial guarantees from those accountants who
are chosen as bank auditors.   They ought to be
compelled to make up their bank returns under
heavy penalties, partly, perhaps, in the shape of
deposits of money in neutral hands, to be for-
feited in the case of fraud or collusion.   As a
further check, no director or director's nominee
should be allowed to hold proxies for the election
of an auditor.   It should be stringently placed
in the hands of the shareholders.   Still further,
I think that no bank ought to be audited by a
shareholder, even if that shareholder be a professional accountant.   The shareholders should
be compelled to elect men entirely outside of their
own body.   By means like these it would not,
I feel sure, be difficult to obtain all reasonable
provisions for an honest audit of accounts,
sufficient, if not to prevent losses, at least to

protect the community against fraud on all ordinary occasions.

The one imperative thing to be insisted on is that these reforms must be submitted to. Banking cannot any longer be allowed to take care of itself, and to run riot without control. The last few months have witnessed what mischiefs may come of this unhappy licence, and to what dangers ignorance and folly may subject the strongest institutions. In the three months that elapsed between the failure of the City of Glasgow Bank and the making up of the half-yearly balance-sheets, thirteen London banks lost no less than £11,767,000 of their deposits entirely through the popular distrust.* Bankers

* The following are the banks in question :—

BANK.	Liabilities on deposit and current account.		
	Dec. 1878.	June 1878.	
Alliance, . . .	£1,621,724	£2,271,852	£650,128
Central of London, .	964,789	1,147,951	183,162
City, ...	2,872,067	3,922,480	1,050,413
Consolidated, . .	2,560,365	2,966,902	406,537
Imperial, . . .	1,807,716	2,434,714	626,998
London & County, .	21,474,916	23,611,443	2,136,527
London & Provincial, .	1,849,222	1,886,027	36,805
London & S.-Western,	1,559,978	1,576,430	16,452
London & Westminster,	21,485,767	26,763,364	5,277,597
London Joint-Stock,*	13,849,586	14,680,863	831,277
Metropolitan, . .	.76,836	318,955	142,119
National, . . .	8,097,794	8,360,920	263,126
Union of London, .	12,398,337	12,544,020	145,683
	£90,719,097	£102,485,921	£11,766,824
		90,719,097	
Net decrease,	£11,766,824		

* In both these cases the acceptances are included in the total amount of deposits.

were loud in condemning the unreasonableness of this distrust; but they have themselves almost entirely to blame for it, since they have systematically refused the people information. Contrast, for example, the usual balance-sheet of the London and Westminster Bank with that compiled by the *Economist* from the figures given in the chairman's recent speech, and you will see at once how utterly insufficient the ordinary figures are.* Other banks habitually behave even worse to the public in this respect than the London and Westminster, and the consequence is that when any large failure occurs people are unable to discriminate. Rumour works on their ignorant fears, and they believe

---

* The following is the balance-sheet given to the shareholders at the London and Westminster Bank meeting :—

LONDON AND WESTMINSTER BANK, 31ST DECEMBER, 1878.

Dr.			Cr.	
To proprietors for paid-up capital,	£2,000,000	By cash in hand and at Bank of England, . . .	£3,427,501
To amount due by the bank on deposits, circular notes and other moneys, including rebate on bills discounted not yet due, .	£21,485,767	By Government stock, .	3,197,973
		By securities guaranteed by the Government of India, . .	£1,150,000
To cash against East Indian security as *per contra*, . .	900,000	By Metropolitan stock, colonial bonds, and railway debenture and preference stocks, . . .	761,151
	*22,385,767		1,911,151
To rest or surplus fund, 30th June 1878. . .	£914,814	By loans. at call and not exceeding 15 days, . .	1,673,975
To net profits of the past halfyear, . .	200,878	By bills discounted, loans, and other securities, . .	15,290,859
	1,115,692		
£25,501,459		£25,509,459	

* This amount does not include acceptances, £719,448.

the worst of what they hear. In this way disasters might well be brought about, which would shake the credit of the nation to its

And the following is the balance-sheet compiled by the *Economist* from the figures given in Sir John Rose's speech at the meeting :—

LIABILITIES.		ASSETS.	
Capital paid up, . .	£2,000,000	Cash in hand and at Bank of England, . . .	£3,428,000
Deposits—at call and notice, say, under £900,000, current accounts, circular notes, and rebate, say, over £12,500,000, . .	21,485,000	Loans and call, and under fifteen days, . . .	1,674,000
		Government stock, . .	3,198,000
Cash borrowed upon East Indian securities, . .	900,000	Indian Government securities,	1,150,000
Rest, 30th June 1878, . .	915,000	Metropolitan stock, colonial bonds, and railway debenture and preference, .	761,000
Half-year's net profits, .	201,000	Bills discounted not over three months to run, .	8,070,000
(Acceptances, £719,000 ; against securities, £1,661,000 ; not included in the balance-sheet).		Bills discounted over three months, ...	545,000
		Loans to customers on marketable securities, . .	4,280,000
		Loans to customers on leases, deeds, etc., . . .	1,157,000
		Over-drafts by customers and country banks against securities deposited, .	830,000
		Advances on dock warrants,	125,000
		Bank premises (worth £578,000),	283,000
	£25,501,000		£25,501,000

On this the *Economist* comments as follows :—'All will admit that this statement is amply sufficient, except, perhaps, on two points. Were the cash in hand divided from that in the Bank of England, and were the accounts signed by recognised auditors, even though we knew them to have been efficiently prepared, we should be inclined to regard the balance-sheet as very nearly perfect.'

With this I cordially agree, except in so far as the 'perfection' of the balance-sheet is concerned, but the astonishing thing is that the giving of these figures was a necessity that Sir John Rose seemed to lament. As if the revelation was of the nature of a calamity, he hoped the bank's affairs would not need to be 'turned inside out' in this way again. In point of fact, the statements made by him at that shareholders' meeting did more to calm the public mind than anything else that we know, and their magical effect is the most convincing proof that could be cited of the folly shown by bankers in habitually fostering a habit of almost thaumaturgical secrecy.

very foundation.   I repeat, no other country
accustomed to banking credit in a highly developed form would tolerate this state of things,
and it must be put an end to at all costs.   Pot-
tering, temporary, and partial legislation con-
ceived in the interests of shareholders alone,
may do mischief rather than good if it obscure
the true issues at stake.

Contrast for a moment our position with
that of the banks of the United States.   Banks
fail there often enough, but rarely or ever does
the failure of one bank, or of half-a-dozen
banks, cause a blind panic 'run.'   Nor are
banking losses at all so severe in the States as
they have often been here in the past.   One
reason for this is, no doubt, to be found in the
smallness of the banks, a characteristic not
without its advantages.   Our banks have in
several instances become so overgrown as to be
nearly unmanageable.   But the main cause of
the more satisfactory condition of affairs which
prevails in America is, without doubt, to be
found in the restrictions under which the banks
work in most of the States, and, above all,
under the 'national' bank law.   As a rule,
even the State banks are subject to Government inspection—not an efficient system, but
one which some responsible audit should replace here.   They are bound by law also in

the State of New York to make at least five
returns of their accounts a year, and in no case
are they permitted to lend to any one person
or firm an amount exceeding one-tenth of the
capital. Under the 'national' system, established in 1863—a system which now comprises
some 2000 banks—periodical returns must be
made to the Government at least twice a year,
showing the position of each individual bank,
its capital, reserves, liabilities, profits or losses.
Statements may also be called for by the
Comptroller of the Currency at any time, he
having authority to demand whatever information may be deemed of value.*

This is but an example of the stringency
with which banks may be controlled, but instances can be multiplied at every turn. To
go no further than France, one may find every
week in the pages of the *Economist* an abstract
of the balance-sheet of the Bank of France,
which puts to shame all the pleas for secrecy and
for the maintenance of the 'confidence' system
urged by bankers in this country. The Bank
of France is one of the most perfectly organised
institutions of credit in the world, and yet it publishes every week fully more than is here asked

* *Vide* Comptroller Knox's report on the currency of the
United States for 1878. It contains a most interesting account
of the national banks, to which I shall have more than one
occasion to refer.

of our joint-stock and private banks twice a
year.   Still more elaborate are the balance-
sheets of the Bank of Germany, issued once a
year ; and I should indeed be sorry to subject
English banks to the rigorous scrutiny which
its balance-sheet implies.   Again, I am told
that the law in some of our Australian colonies
compels the banks there to make a quarterly
return of their assets and liabilities, under oath
of the manager and accountant.   These returns
are, perhaps, far from complete, but it is hardly
likely that they are materially false.   In short,
we nowhere find banking so lawless as in
England—in the country which boasts of the
wonderful development of its credit institutions.
The boast is in many respects a just one, and
in applying the safeguards that may seem necessary to prevent liberty from diverging into
dangerous licence, we must be careful that
nothing is done to check real freedom.   Plain
common sense, however, teaches us that the
reasonable amount of publicity here pleaded
for cannot injure any sound bank, or impair
its just liberty of action.   All that is required
is the abandonment of the take-us-upon-trust
policy, which our banks have clearly far out-
grown.   The intimate connection which they
have established with the commerce not of
England only, but of the world ; the extent to

which the operations of the great trades and the small alike depend on them; their enormous resources, and the constant tendency of these resources to impel the banks into channels of business and risks in business, which prudence should teach their managers to avoid, all warn us that the traditions of the past must be abandoned. We must protect bankers and bank managers from themselves, as well as from the pirates or privateers of trade, and teach them to be content to work within well-defined lines, where, if their profits are less, their risks will be less also.

Such are some of the chief questions involved on that side of banking reform within scope of the law. Unless unlimited banks consent to supervision, or to the publication of fuller accounts, there should be no permission given to them to transform themselves into limited liability companies ; and the reforms here indicated ought to be instituted with regard to all banks, whether limited or not. It will, no doubt, be said by some that private banks should be exempt from the obligations laid upon joint-stock banks. But there is no really strong ground for such exemption. Private banks have of late years been driven to enter more and more into competition with joint-stock banks for deposits, and are affected by precisely the same temptations and dangers. At the same time they offer to the public less security than corporate institutions do in the matter of reserves of cash and unpaid capital. Their copartnery is always changing, and without the check imposed by the necessity for publishing accounts periodically, a private bank can easily grow, as it were, hollow. Death or retirement may take away the support of monied partners, and leave the customers to deal only with men of straw or reckless speculators. Therefore, the private banks of the country ought to be made to submit to the same law as their joint-stock neighbours.

The mere plea of uniformity and completeness, ought, apart from these considerations, to be sufficient reason for including all banks. We have no complete banking statistics, and should no longer be without the means of assessing so essential a part of our national wealth. So far as I can learn, the best and largest private banks will have no objection to compulsion in this respect, and if we may judge by the apparently satisfactory outcome of the recent private - bank failures, none of them should have much to fear. The dividends offered on such banks as the Cornish Bank of Truro, Fenton's of Rochdale, or the Loughborough Bank, appear indeed to belie the somewhat gloomy anticipations of the first chapter of this work. I hope, sincerely, that it will prove so, but we must wait a little before being too sure. When the dividends offered are all paid, it will be time enough to offer congratulations. These small private bank failures, moreover, offer no just test of the staying power of the private banks, which have not yet been actually tested. I trust they may not be so, and, at all events, feel satisfied that the best way to avert the strain of distrust, is for the private banks to descend to the arena with their joint-stock neighbours, and boldly make their position known to the world.

CHAPTER IV.

THE position of the Bank of England in relation to other banks makes a revision of some of its practices absolutely essential to any banking reform worth having. The mere periodical issue of bank balance-sheets on a revised basis fixed by law, would do comparatively little good were the Bank of England account left as it is. In some respects the Bank of England is probably as much in need of overhauling as any bank in the country. Long familiarity with its customs and mode of doing business in some degree prevents us from seeing its defects. And some of these defects arise from changes brought about by time, and cannot, perhaps, be cured by anything that the law could do. As an instance of such we may note the unsatisfactory relation which this bank as a private institution holds towards the outside money market. The other banks have overwhelmed it, so it no longer leads, but follows. Thus it has ceased to be that efficient protector of the bullion

reserve of the country which it once was. And
for much the same reason it has nearly ceased
to be a discounting bank except by fits and
starts. For the present, however, we are concerned with the Bank of England in one aspect
only. We must, in the meantime, set aside all
except incidental reference to its position as a
note-issuing bank, or to its powers and privileges
as the banker of the Government. Doubtless
these functions and privileges have given it a
power, and drawn down upon it obligations
which it would never otherwise have had. But
when all is said, the Bank of England is, in its
essentials, merely an ordinary English bank,
doing, as far as may be, ordinary business. As
an ordinary bank, however, it possesses one
peculiar feature which is of more importance in
any discussion of banking reform than all the
others put together. Through being the Government bank, and for long the supreme bank
in the country in point of resources, as well as
from its note-issuing privileges, the Bank of
England has always been the 'bankers' bank.'
It keeps the spare cash—the coin-reserve of all
the banks in the country, as well as the actual
working balances of the other Clearing-house
bankers. This is obviously a most important
function. If well performed it should add
greatly to the stability of the other banks; but

if done badly, the whole banking credit of the country may be undermined.

There is great reason for fearing that the Bank of England does not perform this function well. There are, it is true, but slender means of judging how far it may go astray from the only safe course in such a case, but still an estimate can be formed ; and, as we shall see, the Bank of England may turn out to be an exceedingly unsatisfactory custodian of the national banking reserve. Attention has again and again been drawn to this subject ; but people have been so accustomed to assume that the Government will permit the Bank to manufacture money when necessity arises, that no effort at reform has ever prospered. An indifference prevails on the subject which few could feel were the real dangers of the situation clearly before their minds.

It is, for example, a remarkable fact that no effort has ever been made to compel the Bank of England to separate the money of its private customers from that of the other banks. Once a year, about five months after date, a return is made to Parliament, which separates the ' bankers' balances ' from the other money in the Bank of England ; but for all practical purposes that return is useless. All that it does is to convince those who see the figures—

a comparatively small number—that the position of the Bank of England towards the other banks is about as unsatisfactory as it could well be. It neither acts as a check upon the reckless lending of other banks in times of business inflation, nor as a genuine preserver of their credit in times of doubt and depression. Were the 'weekly returns' issued by the Bank of England to set forth the 'bankers' balances' as a separate item, people would at once see how these banks were working, and would be able to forecast in some measure the dangers towards which the banks might at any time be drifting. The very fact that nothing is known about the state of the national Reserve, except in an indirect way through the amount of the note reserve in the banking department, is sufficient condemnation of the present custom of secrecy. It is a custom which is, I am persuaded, fraught with the greatest dangers to the community. In the first place, it permits the Bank of England to use at its own pleasure the bankers' money entrusted to it for its own ordinary business. The Bank can without check or question asked use this reserve money to an extent which brings it into the position of having no cash reserve against its own private liabilities at all, in which case it must, if unsupported, prove in a time of crisis to be about the most insolvent bank in England. Any extreme pressure causing other banks to withdraw their money, would at once drain it of all its resources, and leave it with a mass of unrealisable securities. The business of the country might thus be brought to a standstill, and the Bank of England be declared bankrupt. In the second place, the same result might be brought about by the outside banks trading on the Bank of England's published note reserve as if it were all their own. Their keen competition for profits, and the spur of deposit money, tend to induce all banks to work on an extremely narrow margin of cash, and they consequently depend practically, almost wholly, on the Bank of England reserve for any extra supply. It may thus sometimes occur that the reserve in the banking department does not cover by several millions the cash actually deposited in the Bank of England by other banks for safe keeping. Or in times of inflation it may happen that the outside banks deplete their reserve to an unsafe extent. In that case they probably drive the Bank of England out of the market by underbidding it, and, as it were, take away its own money in order to carry on their business. Within the past few years we have had both extremes to some extent, and as a result the situation has been mischievously unsound.

In order to try to discover practically what this habit of secrecy in regard to the national banking Reserve may mean, let us endeavour to make an estimate of the position of the Bank of England in relation to the other banks at the end of last year.   It can only be an estimate, for the data afforded by the half-yearly balance-sheets are of the most meagre description.   Only two of the London banks separate their cash in hand from cash in the Bank of England; and we are therefore, as usual, driven to guessing.   I have, however, taken the figures of the two banks which show their Bank of England reserve as an approximate guide to the proportions held in hand and at the Bank by the other institutions, and the result is the following table :—

BANKS.	Cash in hand and at Bank of England on Decr. 31.	Approximate proportion of this cash at the Bank of England.
Alliance, ...	£203,778	£135,000
Central of London, .	232,210	155,000
City, ...	725,484	537,220 *
Consolidated, . .	666,518	440,000
Imperial, . . .	518,844	345,000
London and County,	3,339,697	2,224,000
London and Provincial, .	420,037 †	280,000
London and S.-Western, .	483,546	322,000
London and Westminster,	3,427,502	2,285,000
London Joint-Stock,	1,862,672	1,242,000
Metropolitan, . .	47,759	32,000
Union of London, .	3,777,143	2,306,667 *
	£15,705,190	£10,303,887

* In both these instances the actual cash reserve at the Bank of England is separately stated.

† The balance-sheet of this bank makes no reference to the existence of a cash reserve at the Bank of England, but in the above table it has been treated similarly with the others.

These figures are, of course, not set down as strictly accurate. We cannot have more than guesses on many critical points in English banking; but the estimate is not, I think, an over-estimate, and it shows us that these banks alone held, roughly speaking, £10,300,000 at the Bank of England last December. But these are, by no means, all the banks even in London who had money there on the 31st of December. There is besides these the National Provincial Bank of England, which is probably now the largest bank in the kingdom; and, judging by the past figures of that bank as well as by what is known about its cautious policy, it would be imprudent to place its cash at the Bank of England at less than £2,500,000. Further, there are the private banks of The City and West End, whose resources are in the aggregate very large, and whose balance at the Bank of England must be considerable, not only on their own account, but on account of the country banks, for which they act as agents. To place these balances at £3,000,000 more, would not, I believe, be an over-estimate at a time like the present, whatever it might be when the credit machine is running smoothly. But to be moderate, let us place all these country bank and private bank balances at £2,500,000, and then see to what conclusion these figures drive us. Adding these totals together, we get an aggregate of more than £15,000,000, as the sum probably due at the end of the year by the Bank of England to the other banks, of whose money it is custodian, and according to the weekly return of the Bank for the week ended January 1st, 1879, the total reserve of coin and notes in the banking department was £10,306,000, or just about £5,000,000 less than it owed at that date to the other banks on a favourable estimate of the probabilities. In other words, instead of keeping any money in hand against its own private liabilities as a trading bank, the Bank of England had actually, at that date, more than £5,000,000 on the wrong side of the account. With a fact like that staring us in the face, is it too much to say that the Bank of England, judged as a bank merely, and not as a *quasi* Government institution, was practically, at that moment, one of the most insolvent banks in the country? Or could any demonstration be stronger in support of the demand for a change in the form of making up its weekly returns? Weigh for one moment what these considerations mean. For one thing, they mean a chronic condition of unsound banking. From the senior institution

downwards, nearly all banks, on ordinary occasions, use their reserves heedlessly, and hold the
trading community hanging, as it were, over
an abyss of ruin. With 'reserves' handled in
such a reckless fashion, it is no wonder that
banking collapses occur. The wonder rather
is that they can be staved off, or that when they
do occur, they are not far more widespread.

In order to understand the position a
little more intimately, let us sketch here
what a banking friend of mine has called
'the natural history of a deposit.' A man
deposits, say, £10,000 at interest with his
banker in Liverpool or Manchester. The
banker there considers it perfectly safe to lend
£7000 of this £10,000 to local borrowers.
He lends, say, £1000, by way of over-draft, to
a customer whom he considers good ; £2000
to a millowner or shipowner on the security
of his mills or ships ; £2000 to a stockbroker
engaged in making money for his clients, by
holding stock off the market till the public can
be persuaded to pay higher prices for it ; and
£2000 on produce, on dock warrants, or on
bills of exchange. Interest has, however, to
be paid on the whole £10,000, so it would not
do to let £3000 of it lie idle in the till. For
all practical purposes a hundred or two will
suffice. The balance all but that hundred or two

is therefore transmitted to London, and lent
either to a banker there or to a bill-broker, at
call, and treated as cash.   He in turn lends
the money out on bills, or other securities
at call, to the extent of perhaps £2500 more,
leaving as a residuum some £300, which finds
its way to the Bank of England, there to help
to swell the total of the ' other deposits.'   But
even this poor, lean £300 is not all left to lie
in the Bank of England in peace.   Quite the
contrary.   The Bank of England has need of
part of it in its own business, and thinks it
perfectly justifiable to take, perhaps, £100, or
even £150, of the £300 when occasion re-
quires, in order to make loans on stock, or on
such bills as find their way to its discount
office.   As the final outcome of this interesting
history, we find the £10,000 deposited practically all invested in some kind of interest,
bearing security, with the exception of some
£350, or, it may be, in brisk times, when
demand for money is very good, some £250.
And after accomplishing this marvellous distribution of loanable capital, all the bankers and
money lenders concerned sit down compla-
cently with a confiding faith in the ' absolute
soundness of our banking system,' and in the
all-sufficiency of the Bank of England reserve.

Under the influence of this soothing super-

stition, bankers are frequently content to allow
their total balances at the Bank of England to
run below £10,000,000. According to the
annual returns issued in May of last year for
1877, these balances were at one time, in the
course of that year, as low as £8,000,000, and
only twice during its course reached an amount
above £13,000,000. In former years also these
balances were frequently much lower than even
£8,000,000 ; but then, of course, the aggregate
banking liabilities of the country were smaller.
There has, however, been no growth in the
reserve at all proportional to the growth of
these liabilities.

The moral of this history is, that deposit
banking, and indeed all banking, is overdone.
Some check must be put upon the tendency of
the banks to run into extremes—a tendency
which the Bank of England encourages, although it is not spurred on by 'deposits at
interest.' It could not stand that spur and its
enormous weight of capital at the same time.
The question is, What shall the check be ? It
appears to me that it need not be anything
revolutionary. The customs which have grown
up during generations cannot be rudely swept
away. Our banking is entirely unscientific in
its conception and forms, and no amount of
'tinkering' will ever entirely change its hap-

hazard rule-of-thumb characteristics. All that we want or can do in this instance also is to secure publicity. If the Bank of England be compelled week by week to make up its returns, so as to show the ' bankers' balances ' in its keeping, a most salutary and powerful check on reckless over-employment of banking capital will be at once provided. Without this reform, indeed, the changes proposed in the balance-sheets of other banks would be in a large measure inefficient. The weekly figures of the bankers' reserve are a necessary corollary to improved balance-sheets, and they ought to be made public. If we, for example, make up the last return for 1878, so as to show these bank balances, we shall obtain some idea of the good that the constant publication of such a return would do. Here are the figures as now given by the Bank :—

THE BANK OF ENGLAND.
BANKING DEPARTMENT.

Proprietors' capital,	. . £14,553,000	Government Securities,	. £14,720,223	
Rest,	. . . 3,312,545	Other Securities,	29,119,440	
Public Deposits,*	4,940,137	Notes,	. . 9,408,480	
Other Deposits, .	31,118,758	Gold and Silver Coin,	. . 897,871	
Seven - day and other Bills,	. 221,574			
	£54,146,014		£54,146,014	

* Including Exchequer, Savings Banks, Commissioners of National Debt, and Dividend Accounts.

January 2.   FRANK MAY, *Chief Cashier.*

And the following table shows the same figures separated, as they ought to be, if the Bank of England is to continue to fulfil its functions as the keeper of the banking reserve of the country :—

AMENDED FORM OF BANK OF ENGLAND WEEKLY RETURN.

BANKING DEPARTMENT.

LIABILITIES.		ASSETS.	
Proprietors' Capital,	£14,553,000	Government Securities	
Rest, . . .	3,312,545	purchased, .	£12,720,223
Public Deposits,	4,940,137	Temporary Loans to	
Private Customers'		the Government,	2,000,000
Balances, .	15,818,758	Other Stocks pur-	
Bankers' Balances,	15,300,000	chased, . .	18,000,000
Seven-day and other		Bills Discounted,	3,000,000
Bills, . .	221,574	Loans on Bills, .	5,000,000
		Advances on Stocks,	3,119,440
		Notes, . .	9,408,480
		Gold and Silver Coin,	897,871
	£54,146,014		£54,146,014

It will be observed that this amended form of return makes some changes in addition to that setting forth the bankers' money. To these I shall revert later on. Confining the attention in the meantime to this one item, let us try to estimate the influence it might have on banking if made compulsory every week. At the particular date chosen for illustration, it is difficult to say what the exact effect of a return like that would have had upon the public mind. I am disposed to think that it would have reassured people, so far as the outside banks were concerned, but it might have alarmed them about the Bank of England. People would have said,—If we draw our money from the banks, there will be a suspension of the Bank Act, for the Bank of England has not enough money on hand to pay the other bankers out. And a suspension of the Bank Act is the usual end of such a state of affairs. We have been saved from it in the late crisis merely by the dulness of business, and the comparatively limited *necessary* demand for accommodation. Had the City of Glasgow and other bank failures occurred when trade was in full career, the suspension of the Bank Act would have followed as a matter of course. Its non-suspension was therefore due to the slackness and unprofitableness of business. Surely this cannot be deemed a satisfactory position by anybody ; and since we cannot alter our banking habits, we must, so to say, put the drag on. The weekly exhibit of what the Bank of England owes other banks would, in all likelihood, prove a very efficient drag upon highly speculative banking. It would, for one thing, compel the maintenance of a much larger reserve, and that in turn would help to prevent the flooding of the market with millions of money that ought to be kept in hand, and to restrain that competition which

is always driving discount rates down to the
point where the export of bullion sets in.
As banking is now carried on, there is a
constant tendency for the value of money to
run to extremes. Directly bankers and others
get over a scare, during which they all
hold the purse strings tight, they rush into
the market and outbid each other for business,
with every penny they can scrape. Under
this competition rates recede, and, especially
if business be slack, money may in a few weeks
pass from a state of extreme tension and high
banking profits to one of diseased profusion.
This happened in the crisis at the end of last
year. For a few weeks, money ruled at rates
varying from 6 to 8 and 9 per cent., but directly the New Year was turned, and bankers
felt they were somewhat more at ease as
well as free from scrutiny, rates fell away,
until by the end of January discounting was
done at less than 3 per cent. This could
hardly occur did every week reveal to the
nation what the bankers were keeping by way
of reserve, for these bankers would not dare to
deplete that reserve to the extent they now
do with impunity. The accommodation given
by the banks would no doubt be less under this
system than it is now, and the profits might
also be less, though that is doubtful, but

all these drawbacks could be endured with equanimity for the sake of greater financial stability. There is no greater curse to our trade at present than the reckless lending to all kinds of borrowers which prevails, and few more pernicious habits than the habit of paying huge bank dividends. In no other country in the world do banks yield returns such as they give here, not even in countries like the United States, where the value of money is, as a rule, much higher than with us. This reform in the mode of treating the bankers' balances is therefore one which must be insisted upon at any cost, as the readiest and simplest means of affording some check to our banking recklessness, and as a complement of the universal half-yearly balance-sheets which all banks should be compelled by law to furnish under audit.

This, however, is not all that we must demand from the Bank of England. It is a joint-stock trading bank just like its neighbours, and ought to be made to conform to the law in the same way as its neighbours. If they are to be compelled to publish half-yearly balance-sheets, it must not be allowed wholly to avoid a similar obligation. At present it publishes nothing except the imperfect weekly return, and outsiders have the dimmest possib'e con-

ception of the extent and character of its operations. To make reform in this direction complete, this return will have to be remodelled. And
inasmuch as the Bank of England has features
in its business due to its Government connection which no other bank has, certain special
items ought to be set out in its weekly return,
both as a help to the market in following the
movements of credit, and as compensation for
the absence of a half-yearly balance-sheet.

A common fallacy attributes to the Bank of
England a large bill discounting business, whereas in point of fact its bills form but a small part
of its assets in ordinary times. In former years
it included these separately in its annual Parliamentary return, but since 1857 I believe that
practice has been discontinued. On referring
back to the figures for that and previous years,
I find that this item of account frequently ranks
below £2,500,000, and for many years averaged
from £4,000,000 to £5,000,000. Occasionally
in panic times, or when the bank had by some
special cause obtained temporary control of the
outside money market, the amounts under discount would rise to £8,000,000 or £9,000,000,
and in the panic of 1857 they rose one week
to nearly £18,000,000; but these exceptional
times must only be taken as proving the rule.
In ordinary times the Bank of England dis-

counts little, and of late years has probably done less business in this way than formerly. It would not surprise one to find that the assets under this head were frequently nearer £1,000,000 than £3,000,000 during the past four or five years.

The Bank of England, however, frequently lends a good deal of money on bills pawned with it by bankers and bill discounters outside, and as the pawning always, when it becomes extensive, indicates pressure on the outside market, the items 'discounts' and 'pawned bills' ought to be clearly separated in the weekly return.

In like manner, the extent to which the Bank of England traffics in stock ought to be distinguished. I am far from saying that it is wrong for the Bank to do this. On the contrary, there are many reasons fairly adducible in support of the practice, not the least being the absolute immunity of the Bank from anything like a run on its deposits. But all the same this business ought not to be hid, were it for no other reason than that afforded by the necessity for keeping the bankers' reserve intact. The bankers' money is always liable to be withdrawn, and it would be far better for the banking credit of the country were the Bank of England to charge the individual institutions a

commission for keeping their reserves, than
that it should invest any portion of the money
in stocks, however good the stocks might be.

Apart from this special plea there is the
strong one of general utility. As now framed
the greatest monetary experts of the City have
often the utmost difficulty in determining
what the present return means, and often
guess wrong. Private stock - dealing on the
part of the bank, trafficking in loans to the
Government, in pawned bills, in temporary
advances on the security of stocks—these and
other peculiar features of the Bank of England's business, are all more or less wrapped up
together in an inextricable way, which is very
unfair to the banking community. Therefore
the return ought to be remodelled in the manner
above set forth. It would then form a weekly
key to the positions of the money market of in-
estimable value, as well as an admirable corollary to the half-yearly balance-sheets published
by the other banks. By this means, and without attempting any revolution in the banking
habits of the country, we should gradually
attain to something like a banking system,
and banking statistics would give some trustworthy information upon the practices of banking credit. In short, if such a change as this be
not adopted it will be necessary to cause all

banks to make a certified return of their cash in
hand, and at the Bank of England once a
month.   That, however, would be at once a
more clumsy and less easily managed plan than
the one now suggested, by which the weekly
return of the Bank of England may be made
the complement of the half-yearly balance-
sheets, and as such the faithful barometer of
banking credit.

CHAPTER V.

In the three previous chapters we have dealt
with such characteristics of banking as may
fairly be considered easily reformable by law.
These, however, are by no means all that
demand consideration at the present time,
and we must now proceed to treat of certain
features in practical banking which cannot
perhaps so well be reformed by Parliament.
Some of these are of the highest, others of
only secondary importance, and amongst the
latter I am disposed to place 'deposit' banking.
In some respects, no doubt, this is a vital feature in English banking habits, but I believe
such changes as have been advocated in previous chapters would in time tend much to
reduce its importance. Should limited liability
also become the universal basis of joint-stock
banking, there can be little doubt that the
dangers of deposits at interest will become
less than they are now. There are, however,
some points in which this deposit system itself

seems to demand handling by law ; and therefore it may perhaps be best to deal with it
now. Other matters have probably a higher
immediate practical importance, but being less
susceptible of legislative handling, come, strictly
speaking, under a different category.

We have seen incidentally that 'deposit-
money' plays a most important part in guiding
the policy of nearly all bankers now-a-days.
They take enormous sums on deposit, and
are hounded on by these deposits to assume
dangerous risks, and to use money without
due regard to contingencies or common prudence. In one sense, the custom of taking
money on deposit at interest may be said to
have bred the high-dividend craze by which
our joint-stock banks have become corrupted.
When people were making money freely,
they lent it to the banks, under temptation of
interest and apparently ample security, and
when trade was active, the banks made high
profits by this money. A bad habit was thus
cultivated which in times of adversity the banks
have not the courage to abandon. They are
determined to make the big dividends still, and
therefore try to retain their deposits, which thus
spur them on towards many dangers. The
spur acts with much stronger force than the
actual money paid away to the depositors as

interest might lead us to suppose, because the habit of looking on deposit-money as money which must at all hazards be used, extends its influence in the banker's mind to all the money he holds.   He practically draws no distinction between one class of liability and another, and consciously or unconsciously comes to regard all the money in his keeping as money which he must somehow, and at all hazards, make profit upon, under peril of direct loss.   Big dividends and deposits thus act and react on each other.   This habit has grown so inveterate, that a bank manager with £100,000 unlent at the end of the day beyond his mere 'till' money, and his meagre Bank of England balance, offers a picture of misery not easily matched.   To have any money in this way 'over,' *i.e.*, unlent, is almost always looked upon as an actual loss of income.

That the mischiefs bred by this deposit system can ever be entirely rooted out of our banking habits, is, I fear, impossible.   Late events have checked the flow of money towards that form of investment, as it may be called, and some banks have, as we have seen, lost a good deal of what money they once held in this way.   Since 1873 the London banks alone have lost about £22,000,000.   The temptations, however, are too great for human nature

to resist long, and deposits may flow back
again directly the banks can afford, or think
they can afford, to bid for them, unless some
change is made in the law affecting depositors' security. Even the change to 'limited'
might merely have the effect of distributing
deposits, not of actually reducing the gross
amount.   Banks would become smaller in-
dividually, perhaps, but, on the other hand,
would in all likelihood grow more numerous.
We must therefore accept this deposit system
as something ingrained in our banking habits
too deeply to be got rid of. And yet a little
consideration must satisfy any unprejudiced
mind that on its present basis the system is
thoroughly unsound.

For one thing, the depositors are always the
first people who cause a run upon a bank.   Its
regular customers who keep balances, and who
it may be get occasional advances, never as a
rule rush to withdraw their money at the first
breath of suspicion. They are too intimately
bound up with the interests of the bank to do
so. But depositors rush like scared sheep the
moment a whisper of danger reaches their ears
and demand payment. At such times the fact
that depositors are supposed to be obliged to
give notice of withdrawal, avails the bank 'run'
upon very little. It dare not allow its credit

to be 'blown upon,' as the slang phrase is, and usually pays at once over the counter all money demanded of it. The consequence is that these very persons whose money may have impelled a bank into taking dangerous risks, are usually the first to cause its stoppage. I believe that no thoroughly sound bank has ever yet been pulled down by a depositors' scare; but that does not alter the fact that a liability of this kind involves a danger of embarrassment such as at times puts a strain on all banks. Indian and Colonial banks get over this difficulty to some degree by taking deposits at long dates— for one, two, or three, even five years, but in the end their safeguard in this respect may prove their snare. The same or even greater impulsion is given to them to take risks outside legitimate banking business, for they usually engage to pay fixed and tolerably high rates of interest for the money, and they have no fear of a 'run' before their eyes, such as in the case of home banks, may occasionally act as a check. It is by no means improbable, therefore, that these Indian and Colonial banks may ultimately prove to be less sound and more in danger from their depositors than the banks at home.

Be that as it may, does not the fact seem strange, that precisely those people who enjoy

advantages from banking without taking any
of its risks, should be the very people to
whom a bank may, both directly and indirectly,
owe much of its troubles ? In other words,
is not the relation of a bank to its depositors
a false one, which nothing but an inflated system of credit would tolerate. Let us return
to the City of Glasgow Bank, in order to see
by means, as it were, of the misery it has
caused, what the position of depositors actually
implies. That bank was due at the date of its
stoppage about £8,800,000 on deposits and
current-account balances mostly bearing interest,
and on the average its debts under this head
had been about as much for a series of years.
During all that time, therefore, the owners of
this money had received a considerable sum
annually in the shape of interest, supposed to
be paid out of the profits of the bank. They,
in effect, shared in the gains, or alleged gains,
of the banker, and were to that extent bankers
themselves ; and yet, when the bank fails, they
claim against the estate on precisely the same
footing as the holders of its notes, or the creditors on current account, without interest, or as
the holders of the bank's acceptances. Is this
arrangement just ? Can the banking ever be
sound which sanctions such a custom ? I think
not. The more it is considered, it seems to

me, the more monstrous will it appear that
there should be no distinction between the
risks of the depositor and those of the ordinary
trade creditor or note holder of the bank. As
has been very aptly said, a depositor is ' a
sleeping partner ' in the bank where he puts his
money, and in some fashion ought to be made
to share the risks of the copartnery. The un-
heard-of misery and loss which has fallen upon
the unfortunate shareholders of the City of
Glasgow Bank is a grim commentary upon our
banking customs in this respect ; and I marvel
how its depositors can have the face to stick
out for the uttermost farthing as they appear to
do.   They certainly have no moral right to
payment in full ; but then morals have nothing
to do with the customs of modern banking.

For my part, I should be disposed to modify
any limited-liability provision which the Legislature might make for the benefit of distressed
joint-stock banks, so as to cause the depositors
to share the risks. Were shareholders made
liable for all debts of the bank up to the limit
of say five times the amount of the uncalled
capital at the outside, or to any limit they may
agree upon, and after that were the depositors
brought in as liable for the deficiency that
might be due to ordinary creditors, we should
have things on a rather more satisfactory foot-

ing. Nay, were it only provided that depositors must suffer deduction of all interest which
they had received since the date when the bank
became practically insolvent, much good would
be done. The deposit accounts of banks would,
no doubt, be much diminished in consequence
of such a law, but the condition of banking
generally would be much sounder. A provision
of that kind might make a difference of fully a
million sterling to the liabilities of the City of
Glasgow Bank shareholders alone, and it would
not be one whit more unjust than the law towards these shareholders as it now stands.
There is no kind of investment in existence
which gives, legally, theoretically, or practically,
such immunity from risk as the customs of
modern English banking give to depositors.
The investor in consols stands to lose by his investment to the extent of having to sell at a
lower price than he paid ; and the holders of
the so-called ' debentures ' of land and credit
companies are always subject to the risk that the
value of the assets and the realisable uncalled
capital of the company may prove insufficient to
pay them. But the depositor in an unlimited
bank enjoys his interest undisturbed by any
fear. Short of the utter collapse of banking all
over the country, we can hardly imagine a condition of things which would not permit of his

being paid. The wonder to me is, that bank shareholders tolerate such a one-sided bargain. I am sure if the mass of them knew anything about the business in which they are engaged, they would not tolerate it for a day. But that is just the misfortune. Parsons, widows, retired schoolmasters, doctors, and all those classes of people of limited means and no business knowledge, who invest in bank shares, are as utterly ignorant of banking as they are of Chinese.

It might be possible by another change in the law to limit the shareholder's liability almost as effectively as by fixing the outside limit of a bank's capital. Were no banks to be allowed to take deposits at interest beyond say twice the amount of the paid-up capital, the risks of the shareholders would be greatly reduced. But that might prove too drastic and revolutionary a remedy, and it would certainly be opposed by a number of the largest banks in England, as well as by the leading Scotch and Irish banks. The size of many of these banks renders anything like thorough legislation upon this and upon other banking anomalies most difficult, and on the whole I am disposed to adhere to the simple remedies already indicated. Publicity and effective outside checks will do more to limit shareholders' liabilities than anything else, and in time may do more to change the

present swollen condition of many banks than
any hastily drawn law could do.   If, in addition to the provisions made to secure publicity
we have some changes made in the relations
of the depositors to the bank in the direction
here indicated, time may perhaps be trusted to
cure the rest.

There is another point to which we must
turn for a moment before passing on to treat
of a subject which I consider of higher importance than even deposit banking.   It is the
position of bank directors.   Since the late failures, this has been a subject much discussed,
and numerous suggestions have been made
with a view to increase the responsibilities of
directors.   The result of the trial of the City
of Glasgow Bank directors has to some extent
increased the desire for a change in the constitution of banks in this respect.   From one point
of view, the punishment inflicted upon these
directors is considered by many to be most in-
adequate to the offence.   And bank shareholders
naturally say, 'We must have a greater hold
over our directors; they will have to be made
liable for the debts of the bank in some extraordinary way.'   Some would have directors
made liable for the debts of the bank to an
unlimited extent, while the whole of the ordinary shareholders enjoyed limited liability.

I

Others with more reason insist that the quali-
fications of directors should be increased, so
that they should always be men possessed of
the highest stakes in the concern ; and still
others would prescribe certain penalties, criminal and pecuniary, with a view to keep their
directors straight.

Most of these proposals would, I fear, prove
futile.   Some of them would undoubtedly produce deterioration in the quality of directorates,
and others would prove a dead letter.   In one
most important sense directors are like bank-
rupts ; it is almost impossible to control them,
for the simple reason that those most interested in doing so will never take the trouble.
The bank shareholder usually cares for his
dividends alone, and so long as his directors
tell him a pleasant story and pay good dividends, they are left to do as they please.
Hence it is more a matter of accident than
of good management if a board be good and
well fitted for its work.   Were it otherwise, we
should not see so many incompetent, good-for-
nothing persons diligently following the trade
of director.   There are numbers of impecuni-
ous people in the City who draw handsome
incomes from this trade.   You will find their
names on the boards of half a dozen or more
different companies, from each of which they

draw fees, amounting in the aggregate to
thousands a year. It is physically impossible
for them to discharge the duties they thus
undertake, and the bulk of them are probably
entirely incapable of discharging them ; but the
shareholders tamely submit to the imposition,
and frequently find, should they try to kick
a little, that their 'boards' are so carefully
hedged round with safeguards as to be practically invulnerable.

A legislative cure for the apathy and stupid-
ity which suffers this kind of plague to prevail
is hardly conceivable. If you forbid directors
to elect new men to vacancies, they can always
manipulate the shareholders by means of
proxies. If you abolish proxies, the directors
can pack meetings, and the poorer shareholders
at a distance will be completely shut out from
any share in the affairs of the company, and so
on. It is always 'checkmate' against the
shareholders.

There are, however, some things that the
law could do, and especially in regard to directors of banks, which might have considerable
practical effect in checking some of the more
conspicuous mischiefs now visible.

First of all, the law should break up the
'happy family' system, whereby a man once a
director may be always a director. It ought to

be compulsory for a certain proportion of the
board of a bank—say two directors—to retire
every second or third year, and to be ineligible
for re-election for at least another two years.
That provision would not disturb the continuity
of the board, and yet it would have an incalcul-
able indirect effect in checking abuses.   Further, and as complement to this provision, some
effort should be made to make shareholders
take some kind of practical influence in their
affairs, by making them the sole electors of
new members of the board.   It should be provided that a list of at least five shareholders,
holding the necessary qualification, and willing
to act, should be forwarded to the shareholders
a fortnight before the half-yearly meetings, for
the purpose of voting, the two names having
the majority of votes on the scrutiny to be the
new members of the board.   Practically that
provision might not be worth much, but it
would be entirely the shareholders' fault if it
were not.   The receiver of these votes might
also be some person other than the board
or the managers of the bank, such as, say,
its legal adviser, and the scrutineers should
always be two shareholders, elected by ballot
by those present at the half-yearly meeting.

Beyond these provisions there is, I believe,
little that the law could do, unless it were

to render plurality of directorships illegal.
That would be a most valuable law could it
be worked, and above all for banks, where a
director's duties, if faithfully performed, are of
the most arduous kind.   There are many
directors who attend their bank daily and work
a heavy day's work every day in the week, and
such men could not possibly discharge the
duties on half-a-dozen or a dozen boards.   If,
however, such a law were enforced, it would be
imperative upon shareholders to raise the scale
of directors' remuneration.   At present bad
directors, who form the majority, are over-paid,
and good directors are under-paid.   It would,
therefore, be a wise and almost essential corollary to such a law to reduce the number and
increase the pay of directors ; and that is far
more than bank shareholders, or any other kind
of shareholders, are prepared to do.

There is but one other point calling for
notice before I leave this subject.   Much has
been heard about directors' advances from the
banks of which they are the head.   Naturally
recent discoveries have evoked a good deal of
feeling on this subject, and it is in the main a just
feeling.   Yet it is hardly possible to lay down
a hard and fast line of conduct for directors in
regard to these advances.   They may be, and
often are legitimately given, and might, if pro-

perly restricted, afford as profitable and safe
business to the bank as any that it could do.
The chief danger arising from the practice is its
secrecy.   If a member of a board can get loans
from the managers without the cognisance of
the board, he may ruin the bank, but if they are
made in the ordinary way they may perhaps be
safely made.   At all events, the remedy for this
evil, if it be a serious evil, lies with the shareholders themselves, not with the Legislature.
They must judge of this business for themselves;
and if they judge it unsafe or unwise to grant
accommodation to members of their boards, they
must pass laws to that effect, either prohibit-
ing advances altogether, or restricting them to
amounts which may be considered safe.   We
must not forget that some of the best class of
bank directors are men engaged in business,
who have bills to discount just as other merchants may have ; and if these are to be absolutely precluded from discounting at their own
bank, they must perforce carry their business
elsewhere.   Bill discounting is a form of
making advances just as liable to grow into an
abuse, as loans on security, or for that matter,
without security, and a hard and fast rule would
affect the one as much as the other.

The danger of a time like the present is
panic legislation, and I feel sure that any legis-

lation upon this point would partake of that character. What is required is not more laws, but more intelligence and greater common sense in conducting banking business. The mere prospect of a periodical bank audit would practically do more to check abuses of this nature than any legal restrictions which could be devised, for corrupt directors could always find means to evade the statutes, but the difficulty of hoodwinking a professional auditor, wholly unconnected with the bank save in a professional capacity, would probably in most cases stop mischief of this kind at a very early stage. To keep him straight, he might, in addition to his deposit of caution-money, be held liable, conjointly with the directors, for all money paid away as dividends out of unrealised profits.

We must now leave this part of the subject, and pass on to one which, though more vitally important, is yet one with which the law cannot be expected in any direct sense to interfere.

CHAPTER VI.

No part of modern banking has been so prominently before the public mind of late as the
business of accepting bills. The collapse in
Glasgow was seen to be due in great measure
to the enormous extent to which the City Bank
there had carried this part of its business. At
the date of its stoppage, it had nearly £2,800,000
in 'acceptances' current in the discount market,
and the immediate cause of its stoppage was the
impossibility of finding means to retire such of
these bills as were falling due. The credit of
the bank got whispered about, and its paper
was refused, with the result that the bank
stopped within a few months. When the investigators' report disclosed a deficit of £6,800,000,
including the capital and reserve, people's minds
became filled with strong distrust about all
'accepting' banks, as a natural consequence.
In the unreasoning fear of the hour they perhaps too readily confounded all kinds of 'accepting' with the City of Glasgow Bank kind.

A severe drain accordingly set in upon more than one other bank known to have large commitments in this way, and there is little doubt that some of them continue still to suffer. It is important, therefore, that the facts should be known regarding this kind of business, so that, if possible, further mischief may be avoided. All accepting business is not bad business, but much of it is unquestionably very imprudent, and a good deal of it hovers on the confines of the absolutely bad, to an extent that may be in the end highly mischievous. The public ought, if possible, to learn the facts, so that they may act with judgment; and bank shareholders, above all, should lose no time in trying to comprehend the nature of the business which they tamely suffer their directors to commit them to. With a view to throw some light on this subject, I propose in this chapter to try and explain—(1) What an acceptance is; (2) Some of the modes adopted by banks in conducting 'acceptance' business; and (3) To discuss generally the principles which ought to guide us in determining whether ' acceptance' business can be considered a safe kind of business for any bank.

First, As to the nature of an acceptance. At the very outset the reader should disabuse his mind of the notion that an acceptance is, by

the nature of it, a bad security. There could be
no greater mistake. What are called 'acceptances' are nothing more nor less than bills of
exchange, and the word has only by custom
become, as it were, the special property of
bankers' bills of exchange. If a merchant in
London has bought goods in, say, Melbourne,
the seller there would, in the ordinary course of
business, draw upon him for the money which
the London merchant had agreed to pay. On
the arrival of the bill, the latter would 'accept'
it, payable at a given date, and it would then
probably find its way into the money market
for discount as Mr. So-and-so's 'acceptance.'
A document of this kind is in no respect essentially different from an inland bill of exchange,
which a merchant in a large distributing centre
may draw upon a country retailer. It is a
document representing the value of a certain
quantity of goods, which the retailer has bought
at a certain price, and his 'acceptance' of the
wholesale dealer's draft or bill, payable three or
four months after date, is neither more nor less
than his 'promise to pay' the cash for the
goods at that date. In the belief that he will
be able to fulfil that promise, the banker or bill
broker 'discounts' this bill or acceptance just
as he would the Melbourne draft, *i.e.*, he advances the wholesale dealer the amount stated

on the draft, less so much per cent. retained as profit for lending the money.

This is done all the more readily that the money lender has, in addition to the security of the acceptor, the security of the drawer, who is bound by law to pay back the money advanced on the bill should the acceptor fail to do so. The advantages of an arrangement of this kind are obvious enough, since we see that by it the buyer of the goods gets time to sell them again before being called on to furnish the money, while, on the other hand, the seller is at once put in possession of means wherewith to enter upon new transactions, at the cost of a trifling payment to the discounter.

This is briefly the nature and purpose of an ' acceptance ' or bill of exchange, and in their essence bankers' ' acceptances ' ought not to differ in origin or purpose from the bill of an ordinary merchant. They, however, obviously do in many ways differ, and we must now try to find out wherein the difference lies. That will bring us to the *second* point mentioned —the various modes adopted by banks in conducting their acceptance business.

The most patent fact regarding this business is that, in adopting it at all, a bank is at once placing itself, to a certain extent, in the position of the ordinary merchant. If the bills drawn

represent real transactions in goods, these
transactions ought to have been entered into
by merchants, and that being so, the merchants
are the proper parties to draw and accept the
bills arising out of their dealings. They, and
they alone, can know intimately the character
and prospects of the transactions which produce
the bills. It is impossible that a banker can
watch closely the markets in Calcutta, Hong
Kong, Bombay, Melbourne, Dunedin, New
York, Paris, Antwerp, or wherever it may be,
and equally impossible that he can familiarise
himself with the movements of prices in the
thousands of articles which form the objects of
merchants' dealings.

When, therefore, a banker steps into the
position of the merchant, and undertakes to pay,
or to receive payment, for goods bought or sold
by the merchant, he is in a sense stepping
beyond his own business. That, at all events,
is the first and most obvious view, and if he
carries his accommodating disposition to the
extent of *trusting* the merchant with the means
to buy or sell, he becomes a full-blown principal
in the transaction, with all the risks, and a
minimum knowledge of the business.

Here, in a sentence, we have one leading
difference between what may be called safe and
what is certainly unsafe bankers' ' acceptance '

business.   The City of Glasgow Bank accepted
bills against credits or advances of its own
money given to penniless adventurers, and
thereby became a huge trader on its own
account in all sorts of articles, of which its
managers could not possibly know anything.
These adventurers were, from this point of
view, its mere agents, and only became its
masters when the losses proved too great for
the managers to confess.   But a bank may
accept against good security lodged, or against
cash even, and then it at the very worst divides
risks with other people.   Business thus restricted may therefore be deemed comparatively safe, if kept within well-defined and
narrow bounds.   Altogether safe it can never
be, for reasons which we shall discover when
we examine, as it is now necessary to do,
the actual business of bank accepting as now
carried on.

To simplify the matter, it will be as well to
leave out of sight whatever inland bill accepting may go on between country bankers
and their London agents, as also the custom,
prevalent with banks possessed of branches, of
drawing bills between one branch and another.
The bank acceptance, business which really
contains in it the elements of dangers similar
to that made known by the City of Glasgow

Bank, is entirely foreign business, and owes its
origin to a combination of circumstances easily
enough explained.   Confining the attention to
the Indian, China, and Colonial trades, which
are the trades by far the most fruitful in bank
'acceptances,' we shall find two principal influences at work.   One is the excessive
multiplication of banks, and the other is an
equally excessive multiplication of non-capitalist traders.   In a sense we might say that
the multiplication of banks is the cause, and
the multiplication of non-capitalist traders the
effect, so much does the one influence react to
produce the other, and out of their conjunction
the acceptance business has arisen.   An over-
supply of banking accommodation leads to over
competition for business, and when once banks
begin to eagerly outbid each other as lenders,
the mushroom trader is sure to come to the
fore.   Instead of lending cautiously, the banks
struggle for opportunities to employ their
money, and in the struggle, inevitably come
to give credit to men of straw.   Yet, although
this is true, it would be unfair to leap to the
conclusion that all acceptance business is thus
originated.   With our colonies, in particular,
there is a consideration which must have due
weight in modifying a harsh rapid judgment.
The colonies are necessarily filled with new

men, who, by their energy and enterprise, have
risen to the position of considerable traders.
In the particular colony where they reside,
these men may be trusted, because they are
known and respected ; but on the London
money market, their signature to a bill would
be of almost no value whatever. To help
such men, the colonial banks step in, lending
them their names on bills, so as to enable
them to transact their business with freedom.
This may be perfectly legitimate business. A
merchant in Sydney, we shall say, instructs his
agent in London to buy for him £1000 worth
of goods. To cover the cost of the goods, the
merchant goes to a bank in Sydney, and ob-
tains, either by purchase or by the deposit of
security, a bank bill on London for the £1000,
drawn in favour of the sender of the goods.
On the arrival of that bill in London it is accepted—always, I believe, in the case of colonial
banks, by their own London branches—more to
certify its genuineness than anything else, and
handed to the man in whose favour it is drawn,
who then endorses it, and offers it for discount,
and with the proceeds buys the goods on behalf
of his Sydney correspondent. Without the intermediary bank, he probably could not discount
the bill at all, or only at much more onerous
rates, because the name or credit of the actual

remitter would be comparatively unknown on the market ; but by the help of the bank which, as drawer and acceptor both, guarantees, as it were, the genuineness of the bill, or, in other words, pledges its credit for it, the paper is discounted at once at the best rate of the day. This is the best, and, indeed, the only justifiable form of foreign or colonial bank acceptance ; and the fact that there are many such in existence, must prevent a too sweeping condemnation of the system.   It is a system by which honest poor men may possibly work their way up to wealth, since it is one which places the man of small capital precisely on a level with the man of large means in the matter of what are called business facilities.

When, however, this has been said, all has been said in favour of this modern development of banking.   The most uninstructed mind can see at once that it must be an essentially dangerous system, because of the strong temptations which it offers to competing and enterprising bankers, either to grant credits, or to accept too extensively, for the sake of the ' profit ' of the commission charged.   A customer of a bank does a few transactions in the fair, legitimate manner just sketched out, and presently sees his way to ' a big thing,' if only a little temporary credit can be got.   The eager banker grants the temporary credit, and loss results. To try and retrieve that loss he grants another credit, and so on, till in the end the small loss becomes an unbearable one. I am told that this credit-giving practice, without which acceptance business would not be very risky, has not taken much root in the Australian trade, and I trust the information is correct. It is the more likely to be so that the Australian trade has not of late years suffered as some branches of our business have done. The extreme dangers of acceptance business of this kind are only developed when losses become the rule and profits the exception ; and as that has been the condition of the trade with the East for some years now, there is, I fear, no doubt at all that the banks in that trade have become more or less involved. No banking practice facilitates the making of bad debts so easily as the practice of lending banking credit on acceptances. A bank slips into large losses almost before it can be aware of them, and it takes courage to face a large loss once made such as men seldom exhibit.

In well-informed banking and bill discounting quarters, the feeling that losses have been made, and undue credit given, is the chief cause of the present distrust of all Eastern bank acceptances. Men know very well that nothing can be better than a good banker's acceptance, if it is honest in its origin ; but as no one can vouch for the honesty, and as trade is known to be bad, suspicion prevails. Here is a form common enough in the City, which will at once show how impossible it is to tell whether the bill represents anything or not. The names are, of course, fictitious in this example :—

FORM OF BANK ACCEPTANCE BILL.

BOMBAY, *28th October* 1878.

The Imperial Bank of India.

Exchange for £2000.

Six months after sight of this First of Exchange (second and third unpaid) pay to the order of Messrs. John Smith & Co. Two Thousand Pounds sterling, value received.

For the Imperial Bank of India,

A. JONES, *Manager.*

P. WHITE, *Cashier.*

To the British Bank,
Leadenhall Street, London.

The 'British Bank,' on receiving the bill, writes or stamps the word 'accepted' across it, and the manager and a director sign below.

Now, it is ten chances to one if the bill discounter, or the accepting bank for that matter, knows anything whatever about John Smith & Company, their standing, or business ; or, if they do know about the firm, they are altogether ignorant of what may be called the true originating cause of the bill in India. Presumably the bank out there did not draw it of its own motion. Somebody asked to have it drawn in favour of John Smith & Company, but did that somebody pay cash for it, the proceeds of goods sold,

or was it drawn against an uncovered credit of
the City of Glasgow Bank order ?   There is
not the slightest means of answering that
question.   All depends upon the good faith
of the bank which actually draws the bill.
So thoroughly is this the case, that the accepting bank here does not even care to know anything.   Banks doing business in India and
China now almost invariably draw all their
larger bills on London banks, instead of, as is
the practice of colonial banks, on their own
offices in London, and these institutions take
absolutely no means to know whether the bills
they become pledged to pay in certain eventu-
alities, are genuine trade bills or not.   They
trust the banks for whom they act as agents,
and very frequently take large responsibilities
upon themselves, with no more security than a
letter from the Eastern bank promising to have
money always ready for bills falling due.

Does the reader now begin to see the dangerous side of this 'acceptance' business for the
bankers concerned ?   It is a business which
has completely revolutionised the character of
our Eastern trade.   The banks have become
the common capitalists for that trade, and its
detailed transactions have come to be more
and more controlled by a class of men who,
having little or nothing to lose, and no credit

to maintain, are neither more nor less than
adventurous dependents upon the banks.
As such they may make fortunes in 'good
times,' and in bad may 'place' all their losses
with the banks, which, for the sake of a little
extra profit, took to accepting their bills.

It is, in short, to this peculiar development
of modern banking enterprise that we owe the
worst liability of banks to gigantic losses. Revert for a moment to the history of the City
of Glasgow Bank, in order to find a simple
illustration on this point. That bank accepted
bills drawn by private customers against its
own credits, and by thus combining the
modern practice of 'accepting' with the old
Scotch custom of granting advances, practically
unsecured, laid itself open to prodigious loss,
for the very simple reason that it placed itself entirely in the power of the customers in question.
It dared not refuse to 'accept' the bills drawn
on it by them, because the refusal would have
at once brought the drawers down. They had
little or no means outside the bank credits
given them, and their fall would consequently
have revealed the dangerous position of the
bank. And the bank had no compensating
advantage whatever to put against this abject
and humiliating position. It could not even
control the bill-drawing propensities of these

dangerous customers.   They knew their power,
and drew as they pleased, well assured that
the bank must accept the bills and pay them
so long as it had a penny of available money
in its coffers.   Thus the credits grew larger
and larger month by month, and loss upon loss
was added to those previously realised.   The
skill of this extraordinary kind of financing
was, in short, reduced to the level of a primitive school-boy recreation.   All that the adventurers did was to 'whip the top.'   It was
bound to spin while it held together.

What made the position still more masterful
and simple, so far as the whippers of this top
were concerned, was, so to say, the extreme
length and numerous doublings of the lash
which they held in their hands.   It wound
round the top in many folds and 'tails,'
till escape was impossible.   To speak without
metaphor, the antiquated and pernicious habit
of drawing oriental and colonial bills at six
months after sight, enabled the adventurers
who controlled the City of Glasgow Bank to
drag it into trouble probably before its managers knew where they were.   In these days of
business conducted by telegraph, and of rapid
communication by steam, three months after
date would afford ample time for the comple-
tion of business transactions, and there is

therefore no justification for adhering to the old six months' sight ' usance' for Eastern bills. It would probably have been discontinued before now, were not most Eastern banks, to some extent, in the same kind of involvement as the City of Glasgow Bank proved to be. They must submit to be 'spun' by their masters, and if they attempted to shorten the lash, whipper and whipped might in some cases come to grief together.

The business grows up to the dangerous point in some such manner as the following. A bank grants, we shall suppose, an uncovered credit of £50,000 to a firm possessing a capital perhaps of £10,000, and either draws for the firm, if the bank is abroad, or permits the firm to draw to that amount. Bills, let us suppose, are drawn by the firm itself and accepted by the bank, and for a time all goes well. Big profits and handsome commissions are realised, and nothing could be more satisfactory to the bank proprietors. By-and-by the current changes : losses are realised instead of profits, and, in the ordinary course of things, the firm would have to go to the bank and say,—'We have lost £10,000 or £20,000 of your money, besides our own capital, and must stop.' That, however, would be unpleasant news, and the firm probably does

nothing of the kind. The ' six months' usance '
for Eastern bills puts the power to conceal its
losses in its grasp, and it usually elects to do so.
Nothing, indeed, can be easier : the firm has
only to increase its commitments.   It begins to
buy and sell recklessly for larger and larger
amounts, without paying any regard to profit or
petty considerations of that kind, and at the
end of a couple of years say, it may probably
succeed in making the loss £200,000, if trade
continues adverse.   Once such a respectable
height of insolvency has been reached, the bank
may, perhaps, be told the truth, because the
chances are that it will then submit to fall into
the position of the top to be spun.   But how
can a firm with a bank credit of only £50,000
get into debt £200,000 without the knowledge
of the bank ?   The process is simplicity itself.
Suppose the firm finds that at the end of a certain year's operations it has lost £10,000, that
it feels bound to hide that loss from the bank, it
will first of all see how many bills it has out.   Let
us say that it finds £60,000 in circulation in the
form of acceptances by the crediting bank, and
that of this £60,000, £20,000 falls due in one
month's time, £20,000 in three months' time,
and £20,000 in four months' time on the
average.   Should the firm's business remain on
its existing footing, it might probably be able to

pay the first series with proceeds of a new series
created on fresh transactions, and the second
series by still another creation on still further new
business ; but by the time the third series was
reached there might be no more money, and
the bank would have to be applied to for more
credit, with the result, perhaps, that the firm
would be forced to suspend payments. But if
the firm chooses to increase its shipments, say,
of cotton goods, to Calcutta or to Shanghai, all
this danger may be for a considerable time
avoided. Instead of buying each month £20,000
worth of goods, for which it gives its acceptances at six months' sight, it begins to buy
£30,000, and then £40,000, and £50,000
worth. By this means the firm has £30,000,
£40,000, and £50,000 worth of securities,
instead of the usual £20,000, to cover the bank
for the advance it makes, and whether the
transactions yield a loss or a profit, is placed
in ample funds to meet the threatened deficiency on the earlier bills as they fall due.
The accepting and credit-giving bank need for
a time know nothing of the motives of this augmented business. To its managers the increase
in the volume of business done is of course
represented as increased and most flourishing
trade, and as all is regular and above board, the
game goes merrily on. Losses get piled on the

top of losses, until we can imagine the following colloquy between the partners of the modest firm on balance-sheet day :--

Thompson.—' How much have we lost last year, do you say, Brown ? '

Brown.—' Fifty-five thousand pounds.'

Thompson.—' Not more than that. Why, what does that make altogether ? '

Brown.—' Well, let me see. We lost £10,000 in 1874 ; £15,000 in 1875 ; £9000 in 1876 ; and £35,000 in 1877. It just makes £104,000.'

Thompson.—' Does it though. That's a lot of money, Brown. How on earth are we to meet it ? '

Brown.—' I see no way except to go on. We must just continue to ship more goods, trusting to luck to pull us through. The bank knows nothing of this so far, as we have always kept the cash turning in to meet our bills so well up to time that our credit is not much exceeded.'

And they probably do go on,—the total of bills afloat swelling like the rolled snowball, till some day a financial panic or a sudden rise in the value of money causes a little difficulty in discounting, when the whole organisation collapses, and the bank wakes up to find itself a loser, not of £50,000, but perhaps of £500,000. Without the facilities given by the ' six months'

usance ' custom for the multiplication of transactions, and the duplication and re-duplication of
credit, this could hardly occur. That custom,
joined to modern business facilities, enables a
speculative firm to crowd many transactions
into the period allowed for the payment of one,
and as money is at once raised by bills on each
fresh venture, it becomes easy to pay the first
series of bills by the proceeds of others discounted at later dates, and these in turn by
still others. All that is required, should losses
accrue, is an increase in the amount of the bills,
and if this cannot be obtained by the creation of
purely fictitious paper, *i.e.*, by bills drawn for
mere accommodation, it is for a time managed
easily enough by reckless enlargement in the
transactions actually entered upon.

There can be no difficulty in understanding
how easily under such a system as this banks
slip into large losses unawares, or almost unawares. They may do so whether they grant
credits or not, if they accept bills on account of
private firms over whose business they, as a
rule, can have no control commensurate with
the risks they run. Hence there is but one safe
rule which banks can follow in this respect. If
they accept for private firms at all, they must fix
a rigid limit as to the amount which they are
willing to become responsible for. An accept-

ance is itself an indirect credit, because it is a pledge of the credit of the bank, and no bank should give such a pledge in any one quarter for an amount that could in the darkest eventuality involve embarrassing losses.

This illustration, however, applies, the reader may say, only to banks accepting for private firms,—a practice not greatly followed in London. The large accepting banks there usually pledge their credit only for other banks trading in the East, and in doing so, cannot be supposed to run the same danger as the City of Glasgow Bank did. There is some force in this observation, but not in the direction people commonly suppose. We have already pointed out that these accepting banks do know, and can know nothing, of the origin of the bills they accept. In that respect they are in fact worse off than the banker who accepts for a private firm ; for if he be a very shrewd man, he may guess at mischief, and stop it in time. But the London banks which accept bills drawn upon them by banks in India and China cannot, in most cases, even guess what the bills are for. The drawing bank intervenes between them and the business men in whose favour the bills were drawn, and hides the business done almost completely from view. It arises from this, accordingly, that these ac-

cepting banks take the bills blindly. They
trust in the credit and standing of the drawing
bank, and look no further; and thus it comes
that some four banks in London are under
acceptance at the present moment to the extent
of probably something like £16,000,000, mostly
to Eastern banks.* I say probably, because
one of the banks, the London Joint-Stock,
which accepts perhaps more largely than any
other, does not condescend to set forth its
acceptances in its so-called balance-sheet, but
the sum is approximately accurate. And it
is surely an enormous sum for only four banks
to take upon their shoulders as a contingent
liability. These bills are all floating about
the discount market, and the credits of the
accepting banks are pledged for their redemption as they become due, at the same
time that it is pledged for perhaps twice as many
millions on deposit. The banks are thus, as

* The four banks, and the amount of their acceptances at the
date of last balance-sheet, are the following :—

The City Bank, ...	£3,267,000
*The London Joint-Stock Bank, . .	4,500,000
The London and County Bank, . .	3,301,000
The Union Bank of London, . . .	4,743,000
Total, . .	£15,811,000

Besides these banks, the London and Westminster, the Imperial, the Alliance, the National Provincial, and the Consolidated Banks accept to the small aggregate amount of about
£2,600,000.

* Estimated on the last statement given, which was for December 1873.

has been more than once very pertinently remarked, using their credit twice over; and,
except so far as the cover they have
received might shield them, it would clearly
go hard with their shareholders did the
drawers of the bills in any instance fail
to pay.   This huge system of bill creating
cannot surely be regarded as healthy, in this
or in any light; and it is a remarkable fact that
the most skilful and prudent bankers in the
city see the danger, and avoid it.   The essence
of good banking is sub-division of risks, and
bankers who receive deposits at interest ought,
above all others, to avoid breaking that sound
banking rule.   Their disregard of it has demoralised our Eastern trade, degraded bank
management into a mere writing of signatures,
and created in the money market a class of
bill discounter which, without either money or
credit, becomes the medium for lodging these
unwieldly masses of acceptances with other
banks and finance houses all over the city.
Instead of being a less dangerous method of
accepting than that of the City of Glasgow
Bank, this huge swelling out of bank liabilities may in the end prove a greater.   A
ricketty trade can be upheld by it till it
becomes utterly demoralised and hollow.

It is usual, however, to reply to criticisms of

this kind, that the accepting banks are always,
or nearly always, abundantly 'covered' by
bills received against their acceptances, or by
securities.   But that is no adequate answer
to the charge here made.   This 'cover'—the
bills and securities given to the accepting bank
—may, in the event of business being unsound,
prove no adequate cover at all.   It may be
a delusion and a snare instead.   In order to
justify this statement, it will be necessary to
enter into some details ; and in the first place,
I shall quote here a portion of a letter from
Mr. W. Rathbone, M.P., printed in the *Economist* of 25th January last.   Speaking of the
six months' usance and its results as affecting
the import trade from the East, he says :—

'It is argued by some persons, that even
in the present day some produce is not
delivered and paid for until the maturity of the
six months' bills drawn against it ; but these
transactions are not in the ordinary course of
trade, and it is to the ordinary course of
trade that the usance should be adjusted.   In
any trade a certain margin of capital is necessary as a guarantee that the persons conducting it have the means to meet the losses to
which all business is liable.   It cannot be
desirable that a trade should be so conducted
as not to require any capital on the part of

those engaged in it; yet the import trade from
the East by steamer now, as, a rule, supplies
instead of employing capital. Drafts against
shipments to Europe are generally presented
for acceptance within a few days of the arrival
of the produce; and if this be sold and delivered
within a reasonable time, the importer has the
proceeds of the sale in his hands several months
prior to the maturity of his acceptance. These
bills no longer resting on any existing transaction, become; as you rightly put in your number
of the 28th December, "to a certain extent of
the nature of mere accommodation paper."

'The six months' usance applied to shipments
by steamer lays, it seems to me, a burthen-
some responsibility upon the prudent, while it
lends an aid to the reckless, and facilitates the
concealment of insolvency. I venture to say
that, but for this undue length of usance, the
career of the City of Glasgow Bank must have
come to a much earlier termination.

' When the drafts on the importers are sold to
the Eastern banks, with shipping documents
hypothecated as security, and when these
banks provide funds for the purchase by six
months' drafts on their London agents, the
evil only takes another form. The merchants
having to discount their acceptances in order
to obtain possession of the documents, the

banks receive the money months before the
maturity of the liabilities the funds are intended
to meet, and the Eastern banks' own drafts
then become "to a certain extent of the nature
of mere accommodation paper." It is no
wonder that most of the leading banks object
to the continuance of the present system, for,
if the holders of large deposits at call are to
continue to accept Eastern paper as an important branch of their business, it is absolutely
necessary for their safety, and that of the public,
that this serious cause of unsoundness should
be removed.'

In other words, the 'converse' of the bill
accepting business may just be as unsound
as the accepting business itself. The same
facilities are afforded, and thus may easily
lead to the same results. It is quite possible, indeed, that these foreign bills, with
documents held as 'cover' by the accepting
bank, may be part of the game of ruin. In
all probability the goods consigned by say
native Indian merchants to buyers in London,
for which the documentary bills are remitted
from India, belong nominally to the very same
people whom the banks may be supporting by
their acceptances. The disastrous fall in the
Eastern exchanges,—a fall due to a variety of
causes, amongst which the actual decline in the

value of silver takes but a secondary position,—
has induced many firms trading to the East in
cotton goods and the like, to try to take home
the proceeds of their sales in produce. They
are therefore buyers in the markets of the
East as well as sellers, and in proportion as
trade becomes bad both ways, shipments are
apt to increase. With the increase in shipments losses also increase. Competition for
produce to ship home, in lieu of bills, raises
prices in the Eastern markets against the
buyer, at the same time that the over supply
thrown by this competition on the home market
sends prices here down. Over stimulation,
due to depressed exchanges, thus of itself induces prodigious losses.

The state of the Mincing Lane markets at
the present time fully bears out the supposition,
that this kind of forced and unhealthy trade is
going on, and has been going on for some time.
Nothing suffices to raises prices in Eastern
products. On the contrary, they continue to
drag lower and lower, and the markets have
all the appearance of a glut similar to that
so long complained of in the import markets of Bombay, Calcutta, and Shanghai.
And what is the position of drawing and
accepting banks in view of such a glut?
They have gathered all the business into

L

their own hands.   The merchants who buy
in the East, pass their purchases on to the
bankers, who hold them as security till
realised ; and the merchants who sell in the
East, sell at the risk of the banks which draw
and accept for them, not at their own.   All the
trade is thus, as it were, forced through a few
channels.   It may be swollen both ways to
altogether unhealthy proportions by the free
use of such devices as I have sketched, by
recklessness, by the very fury of despair,—and
yet on the surface all may look smooth.   But
suppose something comes to stop the career
of some very large operator, and that as a result
the trade suddenly contracts, what will be the
position of the banks ?

For one thing, they must at once become
the direct holders of enormous quantities of
produce.   All the 'documents' attached to
bills, which the acceptors of Eastern drafts
have held as 'cover,' will become in effect
mortgages, as Mr. Thomson Hankey pointed
out in a recent letter to the *Times*.   The forced
retirement of the intermediary operators will
be equivalent to the foreclosures of these mortgages.   The banks must step in and try to sell
the produce represented by the papers they
hold.   These sales must be effected speedily,
too, because the banks have in circulation many

millions of acceptances which are constantly falling due, and which they must find money to pay. Now, there is nothing more certain in the world, I believe, than the uniformity with which banks lose money when they have produce warrants left on their hands. The market always goes against them, be the quantity of stuff great or small. Is there any reason to suppose that the banks would fare differently when they came into the market with £10,000,000 or £15,000,000 worth of produce instead of £10,000 ? Would not the mere fact of such a huge lock up, of such an urgent necessity to sell, stop dealing altogether, and leave the banks face to face with utter ruin ?

I am putting an extravagant and imaginary case ? Nothing of the kind. The figures are before every one, and their meaning can be read with little difficulty. Bankers openly boast that against so many millions of acceptances they hold so many more millions of documentary bills ; and that merely means that they are to this extent mortgagees, holding the most slippery, dangerous, and practically unrealisable security that exists. Thus out of the 'acceptance' system, by means of which the Eastern trade is carried on, there has arisen a gigantic danger. It threatens to

paralyse all business.   Under it the Eastern
trade labours like a dismasted ship in a
storm.   Before it capitalists flee from that
trade as from a threatened plague.

In this view of the matter I have, indeed,
taken the most favourable standpoint.   It has
been assumed that the accepting banks always
hold full nominal 'cover,' although it may be
of a delusive kind.   But do they always hold
even such 'cover'?   I believe not.   On the
contrary, it is a common enough practice to
accept for an Eastern bank on a mere letter of
guarantee.   The Eastern bank says, 'We engage to provide the money at such-and-such
dates to meet your acceptance of our drafts
within such another date;' and on this basis
the business goes on, reaching the gigantic
proportions we see.   The bankers cannot
know the kind of trade that is being done.
They are utterly unable to follow or judge of
the markets.   They 'trust' each other's 'credit,'
shut their eyes, and say, 'All is well.'   Under
the facilities of the 'six months' usance,' all
the paper they create may be rapidly degener-
ating into mere 'accommodation' paper, but
they know nothing of that.   Goods continue
to be shipped both ways in large, probably
in augmenting quantities, and that is surely
enough.   Whether the goods are shipped at

a profit or not appears to be no part of the
bankers' business to ascertain.   A more utter
demoralisation it is impossible to imagine.   No
wonder that the private capitalists have one
by one been for years withdrawing from the
trade.   Still less is it to be wondered at that
firms fail, and sink out of sight, without apparently leaving any gap.   The banks hide the
losses and go quietly on their way.   Where,
for example, are the losses hidden of such a
firm as Messrs. Nursey, Kessowjee, & Company, which failed the other week in Bombay
for something like half a million sterling?
From all that is known publicly, one would
think that such firms exploded in the air like
a bombshell, making a noise but hurting nobody.   But it will not always be so.   There
is too much reason to fear that if the mischief
be not speedily stopped, the City of Glasgow
Bank will not be the only victim of depressed
Eastern exchanges and of trade carried on at
a loss.

   It is impossible to leave this subject without turning again to an unhappy product of
this modern development of banking touched
on above.   The London money market has
been demoralised by it.   Bill discounting has
ceased, except in two or three quarters, to
be done circumspectly and carefully.   Hand-

lers of millions of money like to take what
they call 'big lines,' *i.e.*, to lend in huge
sums.   It saves trouble and makes life easy.
So they gather in these bank acceptances as
being the handiest kind of 'big line' they
can get.   They have the shareholders of the
accepting banks between them and loss, at all
events, and perhaps the shareholders of the
drawing bank also ; so what is the use of troub-
ling about the nature of the business done, or
the origin of the paper ?   Debased by the
corrupting influence of these millions of bills,
that may be mere accommodation paper, general banking business in the city has thus in
too many instances grown slovenly and slip-
shod.   Looking at banking from the point of
view afforded by this analysis of the nature
and character of the 'acceptance' system, and
what grows from it, it is difficult to avoid
the conclusion that one ought to have pro-
nounced more definitely for the limitation
of the liability of all bank shareholders.
That limitation would, perhaps, do more to
stop the curse than anything else short of
the collapse of two or three Eastern banks
and their London unlimited 'acceptors.'   The
paper which these institutions manufacture
at need or to order, would no longer find the
same ready currency in the discount market,

did the bill-broker have to ask the question,
Will the uncalled capital of these banks cover
these bills, and the deposits too, in the event
of failure?   I am afraid, however, that the
actual existence of these bills in such amounts
only affords an additional argument against
any tampering with the present position of
shareholders in unlimited banks.   They must
abide by their contract, and try to mend their
affairs gradually.   Any legislative interference
to limit their liability now would probably
result in bringing the whole structure down
about their ears.

I have dwelt at much greater length on this
acceptance question than the reader may perhaps like, but it seemed absolutely necessary
that the true nature of it should not be mis-
understood.   There is a legitimate kind of bill
discounting for banks and an illegitimate, between which there is no other safe line than that
drawn by the sound banking principle—' Divide
your risks, and lend to all men sparingly.'
The modern 'acceptance' business, carried on
between India and China and this country, and
also, I fear, to some extent between the colonies
and this country, utterly disregards this principle.   The colonial banks, however, have
escaped all share of notice, because they draw
on their own offices, yet that will only make their

danger and risk all the greater should colonial
business become bad, and credits swell on their
books in turn.   In short, if a bank accepts at
all, it should only do so against cash or Government securities; but the safest course is to avoid
the business altogether.   As Sir John Rose
wisely observed, in his speech at the recent
London and Westminster Bank meeting, the
business of accepting is a merchant's or ' mer-
chant-bankers'' business, not the business of
a joint-stock bank, and no joint-stock bank
can go deeply into it without running the
most imminent peril of ultimate, and perhaps
unbearable, loss.

Before leaving this part of the subject, it
may be well to look further at one other point
closely connected therewith, which serves directly to illustrate the facilities with which
heavy losses may be incurred by banks when
they draw all the international business into
their own net.   One most important factor
amongst the many which have of late years
contributed to make our Eastern trade unprofitable, has been, as already remarked, the heavy
and persistent fall in the Indian and Chinese
rates of exchange.   Not only has the fall been
great and long continued, but the fluctuations
have frequently been so violent that merchants,
drawers of bills, and acceptors could never be

sure that business done at a profit judged by the exchange rates of one day, would not result in a loss when the bills founded on it came to be drawn and remitted. These depressed exchanges have been one cause of prodigious losses in the Eastern trade for years past, and must have done a great deal to make the whole trade rotten.

It would take me too much out of my way to discuss the causes of this depression, for they are many; but there is one of the effects of it which directly concerns every Eastern bank shareholder, and some English bank shareholders also. Excluding the Banks of Bombay and Bengal, which, although working almost exclusively with English capital, are both so bound up with purely native interest as to be to a large extent Indian, and therefore dependent for their stability on the stability of our Indian Empire,—there are seven banks intimately connected with our Eastern trade, and with head offices or branches in London. These seven banks have a paid-up capital amounting to about £6,000,000, and reserve funds aggregating nearly £1,000,000 more. They are also liable, according to their balance-sheets, for about £28,000,000 on deposit and other accounts, and in all have thus about £35,000,000 of English capital at command. Now, the

most natural question to ask is, How have
these banks met the enormous depreciation to
which the fall in the exchanges has subjected
this mass of money? Much, if not most
of it, was sent to the East when rates of exchange were far higher than they are now;
some of it may have been remitted thither
when rates were far above par, as in the
flourishing days of the Indian and China
trade they often were. There is therefore
an enormous depreciation to face, and the
question is, Have these banks faced it? In
their half-yearly or yearly balance-sheets, has it
been their habit to write down the loss which
this depreciation indicated before declaring
profits? Clearly it was their bounden duty to
do this, if they were to proceed on a sound
footing, for they might be called on any day to
refund the money deposited with them, and
could have no surety that the exchanges would
recover so as to enable them to do so without
loss. I am afraid there is no bank in the
Eastern trade which has done this to the fullest
extent. The utmost that has been done has
been to write off the losses on such capital as
they had to bring home, whether in the shape
of deposits drawn out, or of adjustment balances,
and some of them have not, it is to be feared,
done even that. Men are so sanguine in the

face of heavy losses, especially when the money
lost is not their own, that the inclination to go
on and trust to the chapter of accidents is rarely
or ever resisted.   Events may justify the hope.
Exchanges may rise and capital recover its
normal value as between England and the
East, why then should severe virtue be incul-
cated ?   It is far better to make things pleasant.
No doubt ; but supposing the worst, what then ?
Would not these banks be in a most awkward
position if called upon to bring back intact the
capital lent to them before the exchanges fell ?
The manager of the City of Glasgow Bank was
not without hope even to the very last that those
New Zealand and Australian land properties
would yet pull the bank out of the slough of
debt into which it had fallen ; and had he been
able to keep its acceptances afloat for another
twenty years, some of the loss might have been
made up.   But everything went against him,
down to the very climate of the colonies, and his
acceptances would no longer 'float.'   They had
become suspected in the market, because the
glut of them had grown too great for even the
hardy receptive power of the London banks
and bill-brokers.   Can the Eastern banks hope
to be more favoured ?   They have no right to
hope so ; and their shareholders ought to see
that they are not living in a fool's paradise.   I

am fully convinced that this also is a most important element of danger in the present state of English banking, and the longer that it is shirked, the greater the danger may become. A weak institution may one day succumb, and drag with it institutions not in themselves weak, but merely embarrassed. Looked at in the light of the depressed exchanges, the whole of the English capital now confided to banks in India and China must be regarded as locked up capital, unless these banks have put aside each year an amount equivalent to the depreciation. Some tables are subjoined which will show how the matter stands. The figures indicate that on the deposits alone of those banks there is a depreciation of nearly four and three-quarter millions sterling, assuming that these deposits originally stood in the books at par.

	Deposits at Date of last Report.	At the Exchange of 1s. 8d. this represents about	Showing a depreciation of about
Agra ; Chartered of India, Australia, and China ; Chartered Mercantile of India, London, and China ; Delhi and London ; National of India ; Oriental, . .	£23,581,000*	£19,651,000	£3,930,000
Hong Kong and Shanghai, . .	4,425,000†	3,687,000‡	738,000
Total, .	£28,006,000	£23,338,000	£4,668,000

* Assuming that the figures in all cases have been taken at 2s. per rupee.
† Counted at the sterling exchange of 4s. 6d., at which rate the capital of this bank is set down in its balance-sheets.
‡ Calculated at 3s. 8½d., which is about the current rate of exchange now ruling.

These banks ought to be compelled to state how they have met this depreciation, which amounts to practically one-sixth on their total liabilities to the public. Supposing they have met it fully, their profits in the years of bad trade must have been greater than those of any home bank in existence. If they have not met it, what shall we say of their policy ?

This depreciation serves, however, another purpose than the mere exhibition of bank weaknesses and locks-up. It gives us some feeble light upon the losses of capital which must have fallen upon those engaged in trade with the East, whether as buyers or sellers, of late years. And as the banks more and more hold the threads of that trade in their own hands, are more and more the controllers of it, the capitalists engaged in it, how can they have escaped their share in these losses ?

That is a question which I must leave those responsible for their management to answer ; but to any dispassionate observer the outlook it presents is not of a pleasant or reassuring kind.

CHAPTER VII.

THERE is but one other subject on which I wish to say a few words. Like so many of those already touched on, it has risen into immediate notice through the City of Glasgow Bank failure; but it is not, strictly speaking, a mere banking question, for it affects many people beyond those connected with banks. The users of bank notes are the people at large, and when a bank with a note issue fails, many people, who never dealt directly with a bank in their lives, too often suffer loss. There may be reasons why we should bestow little pity on some classes of bank creditors, but the holder of the note of a bankrupt bank deserves our utmost commiseration, and ought to be rigorously protected by law from loss. The disclosures which first the investigators, and subsequently the officials of the City of Glasgow Bank, examined at the trial of the directors, made regarding that bank's dealings with its gold, have brought into startling relief the inadequacy of Sir Robert Peel's legislation for the protection of note holders, or in other words, for securing the convertibility of the note. The machinery was elaborate and ingenious, but it has been an entire failure—a failure which constantly embarrasses commerce, and now and then subjects many innocent individuals of the poorer sort to losses they are ill able to bear. It is easy to be seen how this failure has come about. Sir Robert Peel's standpoint was too narrow to permit him to comprehend the true causes of banking insolvency. The able writer in the *Fortnightly Review* for December last says on this point :—

'Without entering upon the long and intricate history of what is known in banking economics as the "currency principle," upon which Sir Robert Peel proceeded implicitly in all his banking legislation, it must suffice to say that the consistent object of all his measures was to limit, and as soon as possible suppress, the circulation of country bank notes, and replace them in the first instance by notes of the issue department of the Bank of England, in the expectation that at no distant period the exclusive function of providing a circulation of notes for the whole of the United Kingdom would be transferred to a single central government office. In common with the authors

and expounders of the currency principle, Sir
Robert Peel believed that it was almost entirely
by the agency of bank notes, metropolitan and
provincial, that credit was deranged, prices
affected, and the foreign exchanges controlled;
and believing this, his animosity to English,
Scotch, and Irish notes, and more especially the
£1 species, was intelligible. The lapse of time,
and the enlarged experience which lapse of
time has brought, aided by persistent discussion
of the evidence of daily facts, has shown con-
clusively that Sir Robert Peel was wrong, and
that the small party who opposed him were
right. It would be very difficult, if not impossible, to find now any person of repute to deny
that it is variations in the rate of interest, and
not any changes in the mere volume of the
circulation with the public of convertible bank
notes, large or small, which affects credit,
influences prices, and acts on the foreign exchange. In directing, therefore, the whole
force of the famous measures of 1844-5 against
the function of issue, Sir Robert Peel committed an error totally without justification in
sound principle, and practically full of mischief
and injustice, both at that time and ever since.
Sir Robert Peel would have liked to suppress
the £1 notes in Scotland and Ireland, but the
local opposition was too much for him. But if

he could not suppress he could limit, and as
regards Scotland the Act of 1845 (8 and 9
Vict., c. 38) did limit the future note issues of
the then existing Scotch banks to the average
of the year ended on 1st May 1845. That
average was found to be two and three-quarter
millions, and for all notes issued in excess of that
sum the Scotch banks were required to have
in hand gold coin. And it will be convenient to
say here that the trade and transactions of
Scotland have gone on increasing, so that for
several years past the volume of notes with the
public has been six and a quarter millions, the
fund of gold coin held by the banks has been
and is about three and a half millions. With a
view to the same end, any new bank formed in
Scotland could not be a bank of issue ; and in
the event of the failure of any bank then existing, its right of issue became annulled. In
1857 this annulment was enforced in the case
of the Western Bank of Scotland, and will now
be again enforced in the case of the City of
Glasgow Bank.'

This extract puts the purposes of Sir Robert
Peel's legislation very clearly and fully before
the mind. He wished to aim at what may be
called a scientific national currency, emanating
from one source, and took the usual English
way of attaining his end. A 'compromise'

M

was effected with local interests which could
not then be offended, but safeguards and
a compensating force were devised, which
it was hoped might make the compromise
work towards the real end in view. As often
happens with compromises, this arrangement
worked altogether differently from Sir Robert
Peel's expectations, and the anomaly of a
large provincial paper currency, based on no
tangible security, grew, so far as Scotland and
Ireland were concerned, greater instead of less
as time went on. Not the least absurd result
of this currency expansion was the practical
working of the gold check on which Sir Robert
Peel appears to have relied as a means of
gradually forcing provincial bank notes out of
existence. Up to a certain point all provincial
banks were allowed to issue notes secured by
nothing at all. They were found possessed of
a certain credit circulation at the time of
the Act of 1844 and 1845, and this they
were left to enjoy. No inquiry worth speaking of was made into the solvency of the
banks possessed of this privilege. There was
merely a line drawn at a given date, and the
banks were told—' Within that line do as
you like, but you must not go beyond it without holding five sovereigns in gold for every
five-pound note you issue.' Sir Robert Peel

may have hoped that this stipulation would
kill off these note issues, but even if he did
so, that affords no justification for the extremely slovenly provisions of this law. No
provision was made by it for setting apart
the gold held as specially a security against the
notes issued. It was merely a portion of
the general assets of the bank. The result,
therefore, of this absurd regulation has been
to clog the Scotch and Irish banks without
securing the note holder, and but for the fact
that, when the City of Glasgow Bank failed,
the other banks took up its notes, there would
have been a great deal of loss endured by thousands who had no more connection with the
bankrupt concern than a man would have with
the Government because he carried sovereigns
in his pocket. The other Scotch banks may
lose money by thus taking up the City of Glasgow Bank notes, and saving the holders of them
from loss, but even if they do not, this is a
state of things which surely cannot be allowed
to continue. It not only gives some banks an
unfair advantage over others in business—the
amount of uncovered circulation being arbi-
trarily fixed by mere chance—but it disarranges
all business. Twice a year at least the
money market in London is disturbed by the
large efflux of gold to the provinces to meet

the term demands for note currency, and yet that gold does nothing to secure these notes. It may even be used as a means of propping a rotten concern for a few months longer, as was the case with the City of Glasgow Bank.

The true remedy for the existing chaos of the paper currency is one that we can hardly expect to see put in force, if we may judge by past experience. There will be again a tinkering, and again compromises, if the matter be touched at all. Yet that remedy is, it is my firm belief, simple enough, and its application should inflict no permanent injury upon any sound institution. In embryo it exists now. The note circulation of the Bank of England has in it the elements of a national paper currency, which might easily be developed to meet all fair requirements. It simply wants expansion and reform. The issue department of the Bank of England ought to be made the Government paper currency department, placed say under the control of the Bank of England, subject to the supervision of the authorities of the Mint. All provincial note issues should be abolished, and notes of this currency department given instead to London banks and provincial banks as they required them. To a certain extent these notes would have to be given to replace existing issues, and as many country banks in

England almost live upon their note issue, it might perhaps be a hardship to demand complete and immediate 'cover' for all the notes required by these banks. To be fair, logical, and safe, they ought to be made to give such cover, but in lieu of that, a small tax might be for a time imposed ; and in the case of private and joint-stock country banks, a rigorous investigation of their condition should be enforced, as preliminary to any continuance of their issue privileges. Should notes be issued beyond the limit allowed by the new settlement, the issuing office ought to be empowered to demand either Government stocks (consols) or gold, as security for every such issue. Without such security specially assigned to the Government, no excess ought to be allowed.

And although making some concession to the weakness and existing privileges of banks with note circulations of their own, a strong step ought to be taken towards rendering all note issues secured, by reducing the free limit of every bank, as well as by providing for its gradual extinction, with the view to ultimately bring the paper currency of the country entirely under Government control. It is a currency that should be made to rest on the national stability, just as fully as the national debt.

The City of Glasgow Bank failure brought to

light a most curious and interesting example of
the value of a well-secured note circulation,
as compared with one which has practically no
security. It had a branch in the Isle of Man,
called the Bank of Mona, and, under its own
charter, that branch issued notes current in the
island. No one lost by that circulation when
the parent bank failed, nor did any other bank
need to come to the rescue, because the notes
were fully secured. The following interesting
account of the nature of this secured note
circulation, sent to the *Times* by Mr. John
Kinloch Greig, the able manager of the Bank
of Mona, is well worth quoting :—

' The paper currency of the Isle of Man
affords, I believe, the only illustration in the
Empire of a note circulation fully protected
by security. The Bank of Mona (a branch of
the City of Glasgow Bank), that carried on
business there, and had a local note issue, has,
owing to the stoppage of the parent establish-
ment, suspended payment, but its notes continue
still to be readily received as cash, and are even
sought after as an investment. This confidence arises from the knowledge that there
are ample securities in the hands of the Manx
Government to pay them, and that until these
securities are realised for this purpose the
notes will bear the legal rate of interest—

6 per cent.—from the date of their presentment. They doubtless will all shortly be
retired ; and thus, on a small scale, at least,
the system may be said to have proved itself
satisfactory, and therefore deserving of consideration.

' It is instituted under an Act of the Manx
Legislature, and the Governor and Council
are empowered to grant licences to banks or
bankers to issue notes on the assignment in
trust of approved securities to an extent
sufficient to cover the amount of the licence,
with the expenses of realisation in case of de-
fault ; and the practice is to require securities
10 per cent. in excess of the licensed issue.
The word 'issue,' however, does not there
mean the notes actually in the hands of the
public, but includes every note signed by
the officers of the bank, so that every note
the bank has in existence is covered by the
securities. To provide against evasion, a
weekly return of the notes, distinguishing
those in the hands of the public from those
in the coffers of the bank, has to be made
on affidavit to the Government, and notes can
only be destroyed and replaced by others
at the sight of an officer appointed by the
Governor.

' The securities assigned for the notes are

usually first mortages on land in the island.
These bear interest at from $4\frac{1}{4}$ to $4\frac{1}{2}$ per cent.,
and in addition to this return for their invest-
ment, they of course receive the current rates
for loans on the sum they are able to keep out
in the hands of the public, which is there
generally 6 per cent. The land in the island
is mostly owned by the men who farm it, and
is divided into comparatively small properties,
seldom exceeding 300 or 400 acres. Such
properties are readily marketable, so that the
mortgages can speedily be realised or readily
transferred.

'An important element, however, in the
working of the system is the very simple
methods of conveyance and registration applic-
able to real estate, and the absence of burden-
some stamp duties and heavy legal fees. This
renders securities of this sort convenient and
reliable, and it will hardly be believed that the
whole legal expenses attending a mortgage
—say, of £100,000, can be carried through
in the most complete and satisfactory manner
by the most eminent counsel there for a sum
under £5.

'These matters, I think, are deserving of
serious consideration at the hands of our
statesmen. There is one anomaly, however,
in these otherwise apparently excellent currency

arrangements to which I should like to draw
attention. In the statute regulating the note
issue there exists a proviso allowing the banks
the option of paying their notes by drafts on
London at twenty-one days' date. Such drafts
when issued cancel notes for a like amount, and
take their place under protection of the securities assigned for them to the Government.
Though this is not taken advantage of under
ordinary circumstances so far as the public
are concerned, it is constantly acted upon in
the exchanges between the banks themselves.
This manifestly might be productive of great
injustice to an individual bank, as, assuming
that its connections led to its having generally
balances to receive, it would be subjected to
the loss of twenty-four days' interest, the stamp
duty, and the risk and expense of negotiation.
On an emergency it might also be resorted to
in dealing with the public, and the bank might,
so long as it remained a going concern, decline
to pay its notes in any other way than by twenty-
one day bills on London—protected, no doubt,
by security, but inconvertible except at a
sacrifice. In this way the notes of the stopped
bank have a positive advantage over those of
a going concern, as they bear interest till paid,
and must be paid in cash. This is a blot
which ought at once to be removed, and the

whole of the notes declared to be payable on demand in gold or Bank of England notes, and I trust that the people of this Island may take advantage of the present favourable opportunity for remedying this palpable blunder in their paper currency system.'

Here we have, in many respects, exactly what is wanted, if our paper currency is to be secured, and it is in this direction reform must run. The present defective and useless method of providing for the currency wants of the community cannot be allowed to exist much longer. They manage those things much better in other countries, let alone the Isle of Man. In France the note circulation is practically an affair of the State, regulated by the State bank, and abundantly secured by the large metallic reserve. In Germany an approach is being made to the same uniformity and the same security by a more drastic application of Sir Robert Peel's principles than he was permitted to try ; and in the United States the failure of a national bank never disturbs the currency, or causes note holders loss, because the notes which the national bank create and issue must all be covered by security lodged with the Comptroller of the Currency.

A most interesting report upon the history and present position of the National Banks of

the United States has lately been drawn up by
Mr. Knox, the Comptroller of the Currency, and
it is well worth perusal by currency reformers
here. The primary origin of the National
Bank system of the United States was, according to this, the financial difficulties incident to
the civil war. A means was required whereby
the successive and heavy issues of national
bonds might be taken up, and it was considered
that this means might be found in the creation
of national banks, with power to issue notes
covered by these bonds as security. These
banks, with their secured note issues, were
expected, at the same time, to prove a
corrective of many evils existing under the
State bank system, not the least of which was
the absence of security for their note issues,
and their consequent restriction to very narrow
areas. One bad effect of this restriction, and
the banking unsoundness it implied, was to be
seen in the heavy rates of exchange which
prevailed as between one part of the country
and another. Business, in short, did not flow
as freely as it ought to have done between
north and south and east and wet.

Some of the hoped-for results of the estab-
lishment of the national bank system have
undoubtedly been realised, although it has by no
means driven the older banks out of existence.

There are still 4400 private and State banks
doing business in the Union, as compared with
about 2000 national banks; and in some respects they may be doing even more profitable
business, for the national banks are overloaded
with taxes and safeguards, till they often fail
to make any profit at all. Sometimes, indeed,
they become bankrupt.

But on the one point of the note circulation,
the success appears to have been complete,
notwithstanding the danger of inflation which
the system might have been supposed to involve. The national banks had, at the date
of Mr. Knox's report, a total active note issue
of 302,000,000 dollars, and this circulation was
secured on deposits of Government bonds of
the gold value of 349,000,000 dollars. On
these bonds the banks, of course, draw interest,
subject to special taxes, as long as they remain
solvent; but directly they fail, the bonds become hypothecated to the redemption of the
notes in the hands of the public. This gives
perfect security to the note holder; and accordingly, although 69 national banks have
suspended payment since the system was
established in 1863, no one has lost a dollar
by their notes. It is on some such basis
that the paper currency of this country ought
to be established, although more stringent

provisions for maintaining an adequate gold
reserve would be required here than seems to
have been thought necessary in the American
Union. In fact, the convertibility of the bank
note there is a kind of fiction, so far as specie
is concerned. The national bank notes are re-
deemable in national paper currency or green-
backs, not necessarily in gold ; and the reserves
which the banks are by law compelled to hold,
are consequently to a great extent 'legal tender,'
and not specie reserves. We could never permit our currency to be based upon so preca-
rious a foundation. Our currency must be in
future as in the past a metallic currency, for
which paper is a mere economising adjunct—
not a substitute. Hence were we to adopt the
United States' plan of securing the notes
issued to the banks by the deposit of securities,
we must at the same time carefully limit the
extent to which such issues should be allowed
to go. Consols might secure the ultimate payment of notes, but they could not always
secure their immediate convertibility, and
practically it would probably be found necessary to keep the same amount of reserve in
gold, which the New York banks, say, are
compelled to keep in 'legal tender' and specie
together, viz., 25 per cent. That would reduce,
of course, the profits made by the banks on

their notes, but it would insure the stability of the national currency—a quality worth a very good price.

Whatever be the actual arrangement or 'compromise' ultimately decided upon by the Legislature, it is obvious that the present unsatisfactory arrangement cannot be allowed to continue. The holder of a bank note is entitled to protection in a peculiar manner, and to an extent which no ordinary bank creditor can claim. To give him that protection, the present clumsy, defective, and confused arrangements must be remodelled. The currency will have to cease to be in any sense a private affair, and, whether it consist of metal or paper, become entirely national.

APPENDIX.

The following is the Abstract of the Branch Accounts of the CALEDONIAN BANK, alluded to in Note 1, Chapter II.

STATEMENT OF MONEY LODGED ON ACCOUNTS CURRENT AND DEPOSIT, AS AT 4TH DECEMBER 1878.

	ACCOUNTS CURRENT.		DEPOSIT RECEIPTS.		TOTAL.
	No. of Accounts.	Amount (with Interest).	No. of Accounts.	Amount (with Interest).	
		£ s. d.		£ s. d.	£ s. d.
Bonar-Bridge,	62	2,572 15 7	489	34,729 15 9	37,302 11 4
Burghead, -	47	1,628 14 8	192	16,549 6 3	18,178 0 11
Cromarty, -	52	1,299 13 3	195	19,535 19 6	20,835 12 9
Dingwall, -	118	28,873 13 1	431	38,614 2 7	67,487 15 8
Dornoch,	40	4,963 6 11	272	20,307 19 8	25,271 6 7
Elgin, -	102	6,889 12 5	202	17,338 12 0	24,228 4 5
Forres, - -	123	8,769 10 0	415	41,494 11 7	50,264 1 7
Fortrose, -	62	3,225 19 1	381	30,139 19 3	33,365 18 4
Gairloch, -	49	1,577 8 10	269	18,620 9 4	20,197 18 2
Garmouth, -	31	2,415 8 0	156	14,066 11 4	16,481 19 4
Glenlivet, -	22	1,108 14 11	106	13,780 6 10	14,889 1 9
Glen-Urquhart,	36	2,381 3 4	97	4,622 18 7	7,004 1 11
Grantown, -	69	2,716 11 1	476	35,562 15 6	38,279 6 7
Invergarry, -	18	2,061 1 11	91	15,824 5 11	17,885 7 10
Kingussie, -	95	4,564 10 3	253	18,473 11 10	23,038 2 1
Lairg, - -	57	4,080 2 10	394	25,836 0 2	29,916 3 0
Lochcarron, -	41	4,581 0 11	336	17,547 2 9	22,128 3 8
Lochmaddy, -	41	1,161 6 4	218	13,570 10 4	14,731 16 8
Nairn, - -	162	7,707 17 8	419	46,051 10 1	53,759 7 9
Portree, -	62	2,544 18 3	243	12,862 7 7	15,407 5 10
Rothes, -	89	2,904 19 3	267	20,808 6 10	23,713 6 1
Stornoway, -	84	3,290 10 11	333	12,760 0 4	16,050 11 3
Ullapool, -	32	1,871 16 11	241	13,136 0 9	15,007 17 8
	1494	103,190 16 5	6476	502,233 4 9	605,424 1 2
Inverness, -	465	62,828 11 5	943	96,831 8 0	159,659 19 5
	1959	166,019 7 10	7419	599,064 12 9	765,084 0 7

STATEMENT OF ADVANCES ON ACCOUNTS CURRENT, CASH CREDIT ACCOUNTS, AND BILLS, AS AT 4TH DECEMBER 1878.

	OVERDRAWN ACCOUNTS CURRENT.		CASH CREDIT ACCOUNTS.		LOCAL BILLS.		BILLS FOR COLLECTION.		OVERDUE BILLS.		TOTAL.
	No. of Accounts.	Amount (with Interest).	No. of Accounts.	Amount (with Interest).	No.	Amount.	No.	Amount.	No.	Amount (with Interest).	
		£ s. d.		£ s. d.		£ s. d.		£ s. d.		£ s. d.	£ s. d.
Bonar-Bridge,	41	8,182 9 6	3	2,881 3 9	477	18,835 1 1	12	283 12 10	50	2,851 3 7	33,033 10 9
Burghead,	18	2,769 13 11	4	922 3 7	117	3,004 7 5	7	1,709 5 5	8	836 16 4	9,241 17 8
Cromarty,	21	6,045 7 7	4	6,613 1 3	74	1,298 18 1	7	64 18 1	6	132 16 3	17,154 8 1
Dingwall,	96	17,862 8 0	24	24,549 12 2	327	31,055 0 9	4	1,833 16 1	64	4,110 16 9	79,411 13 9
Dornoch,	12	4,607 0 11	3	269 14 3	123	3,888 0 9	60	407 18 8	3	61 0 0	9,233 14 9
Elgin,	36	12,847 18 7	20	6,831 12 8	382	22,833 10 2	10	4,198 12 6	7	156 7 7	46,868 1 6
Forres,	64	25,208 0 6	19	18,492 15 11	318	34,440 13 10	27	912 5 8	22	2427 15 8	81,481 17 7
Fortrose,	30	4,257 19 3	14	4,005 2 5	222	6,309 13 10	15	512 5 6	9	75 1 11	15,160 2 11
Gairloch,	10	2,168 14 0	1	196 1 10	41	654 13 1	16	191 5 0	...	......	3,210 14 6
Garmouth,	33	20,241 17 6	3	751 17 4	71	24,144 19 2	2	812 5 0	3	710 12 4	46,661 6 2
Glenlivet,	20	1,802 17 0	2	417 4 0	204	5,284 16 8	2	459 5 7	9	211 19 0	8,176 2 4
Glen-Urquhart,	13	1,996 12 11	1	132 0 0	87	2,129 4 8	5	166 1 5	...	......	4,422 19 0
Grantown,	25	3,953 18 7	10	4,020 13 9	484	12,862 5 9	16	449 17 0	22	647 18 6	21,934 13 7
Invergarry,	14	751 1 6	...	......	21	522 15 8	1	31 2 8	...	......	1,304 19 10
Kingussie,	38	14,230 11 7	3	1,615 9 0	242	20,035 16 4	11	544 16 7	13	216 14 10	36,643 8 4
Lairg,	18	2,267 5 0	1	12 0 0	183	3,680 5 5	10	158 3 10	35	591 4 6	6,709 8 9
Lochcarron,	27	9,223 6 7	6	3,182 11 4	126	7,081 12 1	6	180 2 0	17	2,516 11 5	22,184 4 1
Lochmaddy,	23	1,224 1 6	1	203 13 1	201	2,268 19 7	3	82 2 4	14	736 10 10	4,515 7 4
Nairn,	49	9,941 16 3	13	7,901 8 6	238	12,112 17 4	45	2,004 16 0	35	2,931 7 3	34,892 5 4
Portree,	29	3,946 1 9	...	......	270	4,945 17 8	4	76 4 0	118	1,782 1 9	10,750 4 10
Rothes,	21	1,674 3 5	4	1,474 16 8	207	12,157 9 0	4	694 4 9	43	2,560 2 0	18,560 16 11
Stornoway,	32	6,929 16 7	19	22,534 8 7	204	8,507 10 0	22	488 12 9	39	1,363 10 0	39,823 17 11
Ullapool,	13	1,480 16 9	1	15 6 10	36	888 19 2	...	......	1	3 15 0	2,388 17 9
Inverness,	683	163,613 19 2	147	107,023 6 8	4658	238,942 19 11	296	16,261 10 4	518	24,923 16 6	550,765 12 7
	284	169,477 16 8	80	180,278 13 2	1481	116,747 17 1	...	......	258	14,876 16 11	481,381 3 10
	967	333,091 15 10	227	287,301 19 10	6139	355,690 17 0	296	16,261 10 4	776	39,800 13 5	1,032,146 16 5

OPINIONS OF THE PRESS.

The Times.

' Mr. Wilson hardly does himself justice by the title and professed aim of his book. He examines the economic position of foreign countries as a means of throwing light on the prospects of English trade, but his examination is so thorough that we cannot help regretting the narrowness of his point of view, which prevents him doing full justice to what is really his main subject. . . . But though Mr. Wilson has, perhaps, just missed giving the right impression of the importance of this subject, no one can read the book as it stands without being struck by the information it contains, the wide reach and suggestiveness of the writing, which touches very properly on purely political as well as economic subjects, and the Carlylean vigour of the style, which is at times of an unusual heat and vehemence for a merely economic treatise, though not without its place in a popular and literary work. It is a merely negative criticism that the point of view of such a book is narrow. There are not too many clever and suggestive books, and when we find one we must be only too glad to have our minds roused and stimulated, although the writer, we may imagine, might have been more artistic and complete. . . . But while we are thus of opinion that the discussion of the book is in some respects defective economically, we do not wish in any way to qualify the view already expressed that the book is most deserving of study. As a comprehensive political and economic survey of foreign countries, it supplies a much-felt want, and the style and treatment are such as to deserve high praise, however we may dissent from much of the reasoning and conclusions.'

The Saturday Review (*Second Notice*).

' Mr. Wilson's book is a valuable contribution to the very scanty literature which the important topic of the prospects of British trade has as yet called forth.'

The Scotsman.

'The question which Mr. Wilson sets himself to solve is, "What are the prospects of our future trade?" . . . Before mentioning the results of this inquiry, it may be said that Mr. Wilson, in dealing with the question, does not speak in any half-hearted fashion. He has strong opinions, and he does not hesitate to express them. It would not be wise to endorse all his opinions, and, unquestionably, if some of them are admitted to be wrong, then a good deal of his argument will fall to the ground. But a careful perusal of the work will perhaps lead to the conclusion that some of his opinions are not so wrong in themselves as wrong in the manner in which they are stated. . . . It would be wrong not to point to the fact that the chapter on British India is one of surpassing interest. Mr. Wilson asserts, and apparently proves, that British India at this time is actually bankrupt, and that instead of carrying to the inhabitants of that country good government and those advantages which will ensure to them the enjoyment of the fruits of their labour, we have taken, and are fast taking, to a much greater extent the position of a Government which wrings from its subjects the last farthing of their means and keeps them always on the verge of starvation. It is not easy to controvert the figures he brings forward, and it is certain that the remedy for the state of things he describes involves an entire change in our manner of dealing with India, not only as to her government, but particularly as to her finance administration. . . . This is only a brief sketch of a book which, interesting as it is, is rather melancholy in its conclusions. Nor does Mr. Wilson's dark outlook extend only to the resources of modern countries. More than once in the course of his work he hints at probable great crashes at home. Without speaking very directly, he tells us that the bankers of Great Britain have heaped up securities to an enormous extent, many of which may, and probably will, in certain circumstances, be valueless. . . .'

The Saturday Review (*First Notice*).

' We know no book of the kind in which so much readable matter is collected in a moderate compass. The chief questions, too, on which Mr. Wilson fixes the attention of the reader are the right questions to study carefully. He asks what in each case are the causes of stagnation ; what have been the effects of foreign, and especially English, loans on the trade of each country which has borrowed largely abroad ; what have been the effects of Free Trade or Protection ; and what are the advantages and disadvantages which in each case England will have in competing for trade when and if trade revives. Mr. Wilson has much to say on all these points which deserves consideration.'

The Economist.

' These volumes contain a series of cleverly-written descriptions of the present economic condition of the principal countries of the world, and of the most important British colonies, which now form some of the most powerful communities in existence.'

The Daily News.

' Traders, investors, holders of foreign stocks, will all do well to read these volumes.'

The Dundee Advertiser (*First Notice*).

' Uncompromising vigour is the characteristic of Mr. Wilson's mode of writing. He does not merely take figures from blue-books and reproduce them as bare figures, he always determines what the figures represent. This plain mode of dealing with them many a time shows how fallacious figures of themselves may often be, and elicits results which certainly are not looked for. The author is not by any means a statistical writer. His information is invariably taken from those who are on the spot, and in dealing with statistics his aim is to elucidate their signification and the manner by which the facts or results they stand for are brought about.'

The Examiner.

' There can be no doubt that Mr. Wilson is a careful and cautious writer, possessing a firm and masterful grasp of his subject, gifted not only with a marvellous talent for thorough economic research, but also with a shrewd capacity for clearly drawing correct inferences from the most complex statistical premises. He writes in a bright, crisp, vivid fashion, and hence his essays are never dull. If political economists, as a rule, had the same knack of clear expression and popular presentment of dry facts, economic treatises would rarely be voted revolting reading even by subscribers to circulating libraries. Whether Mr. Wilson's views are accepted or not, his work, rich with the garnered results of patient investigation, full to overflowing with striking statistical " points " and valuable but not easily accessible information upon cosmopolitan finance, must be accepted as the most complete and compressed popular epitome in our language of all that is most trustworthy concerning the economic resources of the great nations of the earth. Had such a book as this been in existence some years ago, when the gullible investing class went madly into transactions in foreign loans without knowing anything more about the concerns into which they put their money than that they promised to yield from 8 to 15 per cent. of interest, a vast deal of misery would have been avoided, and hundreds of happy homes probably guarded from ruin.'

The Spectator.

' The chapter on India is the boldest chapter in the book ; some readers will call it rash, or perhaps by a worse name ; hardly a single point connected with the financial or political management of our Indian Empire but rouses Mr. Wilson's indignation and scorn. We are wholly unable to agree with it, but it is a forcible statement of the pessimist side of the case. Vast sums of money have been expended with the view of opening up and developing the resources of the country, but the results have been most seriously disappointing. . . . After all, we have taken up but a few points, which may, however, serve as samples of this very remarkable book, and commend it to the study of such as are interested in trade or in politics. We could have wished to add a line or two on the political bearing of economic facts, and especially on the singular earnestness of political conviction that runs through Mr. Wilson's work. There is something, we think, of a different fibre from sentiment in the pleasure of meeting with a financier who never loses sight of the fact that all this manipulation of money and what stands for money is, in the last resort, manipulation of the lives and fortune and happiness of millions of human beings.'

The Athenæum.

' We shall indeed see that, wide as Mr. Wilson's survey is, it is incomplete. It looks only to the foreign trade of this country, and overlooks the home trade. He starts, in his own words, with the assumption that " the present trade depression leads to the inference that the real source of it lies outside ourselves," whereas there is sufficient reason for holding that its source lies in part not outside, but, if we so express it, within ourselves, in our ways of doing business at home as well as abroad, and in both special causes affecting our home trade, and general causes affecting it and our foreign trade together. Nevertheless the breadth, importance, and interest of the inquiry which Mr. Wilson follows entitle his work to careful attention, whatever may be thought of the adequacy of the induction from which his general conclusions are drawn, or of the correctness of some of his views on particular points. . . . On the whole, a book of great value, not only for the end the author has in view, but as an example of the sort of inquiry that ought to take the place of much barren deduction in English political economy. And if, as we hope, the solid merits of the work should carry it into a second edition, we may also hope that the author will mend some of his sentences and phrases.'

M. de Fontpertuis in 'L'Economiste Français.'

' C'est la crise sous laquelle le monde industriel et commercial se débat depuis plusieurs années qui a mis la plume dans la main de M. Alexander Johnstone Wilson ; c'est elle qui lui a inspiré l'idée d'une étude des forces productives et de la puissance économique de son propre pays, comparées à celles des autres grandes nations industrielles du globe. Et cette idée, il l'a poursuivie dans une série d'*Essays*, qu'il a publiés d'abord, en partie du moins, dans les Revues anglaises, mais qu'il vient de réunir, en les complétant, revoyant et coordonnant, en deux gros volumes d'une lecture fort instructive et même fort attachante, disons-le tout d'abord.'

The Iron and Coal Trades Review.

' Such a work as Mr. Wilson's will materially assist one to elucidate matters, as his examination of the question is very thorough. and one cannot, aiter a perusal of the work, but acknowledge not only the large amount of information it contains, but also the suggestiveness of the author's diction. He has the subject fully under command, and touches not only on political but on economic matters in a very impressive manner.

The Daily Telegraph.

' A valuable and interesting book.'

The Statist.

' With Mr. Wilson's views on India we substantially agree. His indictment of our Indian policy is, with one or two exceptions, well drawn up. We have over-engineered the country, and involved it in debt to an extent which will seriously injure its prosperity for some time to come. Mr. Wilson does his best to be fair in speaking of what has been effected in India. He is willing to admit that a good deal of the works executed will eventually pay better than they do now. In the main, however, he thinks he is justified in condemning the extensive scale of these works. It should be remembered, however, that great pressure has been put on the Government of India to "develope" India, and that by the very party to whom Mr. Wilson to all appearance belongs, though on this point he disagrees with them, the "philanthropic" Liberals. . . . Mr. Wilson's conclusion is, then, that we have arrived at a *crise définitive*, as M. Georges de Laveleye calls it. His reasons for adopting this opinion are, we need hardly say, very different from those of the able Belgian economist. Mr. Wilson's analysis of the present state of nations is more searching than M. de Laveleye's, and hence his conclusions are, in our opinion, the less questionable of the two. . . . Altogether, the book is in our view most able and suggestive."

The Standard.

' In the nature of things, it is impossible for an individual to conduct satisfactorily an inquiry so limitless. A single country's industrial, manufacturing, and commercial condition and prospects one man may conceivably understand thoroughly, but no mind, however capacious, can master the inexhaustible problems which all the countries of the earth present for solution. Even if Mr. Wilson had devoted a lifetime to his subject, he must necessarily have failed, but the conditions under which he wrote precluded the possibility of even a comparative success. . . . It is no reflection upon Mr. Wilson, therefore, to say that his work is unequal, superficial, and inconclusive. Unfortunately, it is as dogmatic as it is shallow, and very irreverently controversial. The hobbies of the author are trotted out whenever opportunity offers, and not seldom when it does not. This is a fault for which there is no excuse. Superficiality was a necessary condition of his task, but a little self-restraint would have avoided self-opinionated arrogance. Mr. Wilson is a violent political partisan, and full of crotchets ; but crotchety partisanship is an unpromising frame of mind in which to approach the study of economic problems.'

Mr. John Morley's Address to the Trades' Union Congress at Bristol.

' Mr. A. J. Wilson, the author of two well-informed and comprehensive volumes on the " Resources of Modern Countries," decides that the backward wave which has swept the trade of the whole world downwards has been due to causes too universal to lead us to suppose that any special decrease in the producing and monopolising capacities of England has occurred.'

Pall Mall Gazette.

' It is impossible to conceive a more important subject than that which is dealt with in these volumes. This is nothing less than to examine into the causes of the present wide-spread depression, to determine what the prospect of recovery may be, and what effect the whole range of circumstances will have upon the future prosperity of this country. . . . Mr. Wilson seems to have done the work he set himself thoroughly ; and the conclusion which he comes to is certainly as uncomfortable as can well be. From first to last he takes a gloomy view of the situation. . . . So far, we must admit, the course of trade has to a great degree followed Mr. Wilson's dreary forecast. . . . But grave as are the facts which Mr. Wilson has arranged in separate batches, and still graver as they appear when they are all summed up together, we cannot but think that he has been too careful to eliminate favourable chances from his calculations. During this whole period of stagnation people in general have been practising economy. Much of the capital sunk in unremunerative and not immediately remunerative enterprises has been of some service to the countries in which it was spent. Bad harvests in England and droughts in India are not likely to be continuous, and a good harvest at home or a series of favourable years in India would produce a marked effect. The omission of these and similar considerations is a fault, for the dark side of the picture is in all conscience dark enough. Another mistake is the vehemence with which Mr. Wilson puts forward political views of a peculiarly shallow and uninformed character. In spite of these drawbacks, however, the book is valuable at the present time.'

The English Independent.

'All who are interested in the questions may study with profit the ample store of details which he has grouped together on a very intelligible and useful plan.'

The Birmingham Daily Post.

' From whatever cause, our commercial supremacy appears to be menaced, and to those who are disposed to investigate the facts which have a bearing on the present situation we cannot suggest any more profitable reading than Mr. Wilson's able and thoughtful volumes. . . .'

The Manchester Guardian.

' Mr. Wilson has produced a very readable book, and although we think he takes too gloomy a view of the future of British trade, we acknowledge that there is much in his warnings which has substantial foundation. It is mainly by giving heed to such warnings that we shall avoid the dangers to which they point.'

The Nottingham Daily Guardian.

' To those anxious to realise the position financially of foreign countries we can heartily recommend Mr. Wilson's work. Whether they adopt his views or not, they will find in these two volumes an amount of carefully-arranged information hardly to be obtained elsewhere, and a mass of shrewd comment on the causes of commercial difficulties almost more valuable.'

The Liverpool Daily Courier.

' Whatever differences of opinion there may be about the cause of depressed trade and about the prospects of improvement, the essays of Mr. Wilson will repay perusal by thoughtful men, and as the arguments are effectively arranged, and boldly and clearly stated, the book will not be found dry reading by commercial men.'

The Financial and Mercantile Gazette (*a Lisbon Paper*).

' By comparing the above extracts with our views on the matter which have been more than once exposed in our articles on the situation of the country, our readers will see that, apart from some inevitable exceptions, we are in perfect harmony with the ideas entertained by Mr. Johnstone Wilson as to the general system followed here respecting financial and economical matters. . . .'

The Leeds Mercury.

' There is not one of his chapters, so far as we have been able to examine them, that will not repay careful reading, although he is perhaps inclined to the pessimist point of view.' .

The Literary World.

'These articles form a book demanding serious consideration from the statesman and the philanthropist. What, for instance, can be more startling than the indictment Mr. Wilson draws up against British rule in India?'

The Sheffield Daily Telegraph.

' In fact, we know no book dealing with the science of Political Economy which is so well worthy a careful study.'

The Glasgow Herald.

' Mr. Wilson himself deprecates the idea that his work could be exhaustive. We will venture to say that no individual writer could have gone deeper into the subject than he has.'

The Liverpool Albion.

' In dealing with our foreign trade, Mr. Wilson has shown a familiarity with the history of all nations, a knowledge of foreign politics, a grasp of the economic condition of foreign countries in all quarters of the globe, and a power of taking a broad, practical, unimpassioned, and unprejudiced view of things which give to his opinions and conclusions a weight and significance which few commercial writers can command. On the whole he takes a gloomy view of the future —too gloomy we think ; and yet on one point on which the majority of people feel some alarm, namely, foreign competition, he preserves perfect equanimity.'

Aberdeen Daily Free Press (*Second Notice*).

These volumes form one of the most valuable books on trade and finance ever published.'

39 PATERNOSTER ROW, E.C.

LONDON, *September* 1878.

GENERAL LIST OF WORKS

PUBLISHED BY

MESSRS. LONGMANS, GREEN & CO.

———∞⊙⊙∞———

HISTORY, POLITICS, HISTORICAL MEMOIRS, &c.

A History of England from the Conclusion of the Great War in 1815. By SPENCER WALPOLE, Author of 'Life of the Rt. Hon. Spencer Perceval.' VOLS. I. & II. 8vo. 36s.

History of England in the 18th Century. By W. E. H. LECKY, M.A. VOLS. I. & II. 1700-1760. 2 vols. 8vo. 36s.

The History of England from the Accession of James II. By the Right Hon. Lord MACAULAY.

STUDENT'S EDITION, 2 vols. cr. 8vo. 12s.
PEOPLE'S EDITION, 4 vols. cr. 8vo. 16s.
CABINET EDITION, 8 vols. post 8vo. 48s.
LIBRARY EDITION, 5 vols. 8vo. £4.

Critical and Historical Essays contributed to the Edinburgh Review. By the Right Hon. Lord MACAULAY.

CHEAP EDITION, crown 8vo. 3s. 6d.
STUDENT'S EDITION, crown 8vo. 6s.
PEOPLE'S EDITION, 2 vols. crown 8vo. 8s.
CABINET EDITION, 4 vols. 24s.
LIBRARY EDITION, 3 vols. 8vo. 36s.

Lord Macaulay's Works. Complete and uniform Library Edition. Edited by his Sister, Lady TREVELYAN. 8 vols. 8vo. with Portrait, £5. 5s.

The History of England from the Fall of Wolsey to the Defeat of the Spanish Armada. By J. A. FROUDE, M.A.

CABINET EDITION, 12 vols. cr. 8vo. £3. 12s.
LIBRARY EDITION, 12 vols. 8vo. £8. 18s.

The English in Ireland in the Eighteenth Century. By J. A. FROUDE, M.A. 3 vols. 8vo. £2. 8s.

Journal of the Reigns of King George IV. and King William IV. By the late C. C. F. GREVILLE, Esq. Edited by H. REEVE, Esq. Fifth Edition. 3 vols. 8vo. price 36s.

The Life of Napoleon III. derived from State Records, Unpublished Family Correspondence, and Personal Testimony. By BLANCHARD JERROLD. In Four Volumes, 8vo. with numerous Portraits and Facsimiles. VOLS. I. to III. price 18s. each.

The Constitutional His-tory of England since the Accession of George III. 1760 1870. By Sir THOMAS ERSKINE MAY, K.C.B. D.C.L. Fifth Edition. 3 vols. crown 8vo. 18s.

Democracy in Europe; a History. By Sir THOMAS ERSKINE MAY, K.C.B. D.C.L. 2 vols. 8vo. 32s.

A

Introductory Lectures on Modern History delivered in 1841 and 1842. By the late Rev. T. ARNOLD, D.D. 8vo. price 7s. 6d.

On Parliamentary Go- vernment in England; its Origin, Development, and Practical Operation. By ALPHEUS TODD. 2 vols. 8vo. price £1. 17s.

History of Civilisation in England and France, Spain and Scotland. By HENRY THOMAS BUCKLE. 3 vols. crown 8vo. 24s.

Lectures on the History of England from the Earliest Times to the Death of King Edward II. By W. LONGMAN, F.S.A. Maps and Illustrations. 8vo. 15s.

History of the Life & Times of Edward III. By W. LONG-MAN, F.S.A. With 9 Maps, 8 Plates, and 16 Woodcuts. 2 vols. 8vo. 28s.

History of the Life and Reign of Richard III. To which is added the Story of PERKIN WARBECK, from Original Documents. By JAMES GAIRDNER. With Portrait and Map. Crown 8vo. 10s. 6d.

The Life of Simon de Montfort, Earl of Leicester, with special reference to the Parliamentary History of his time. By G. W. PROTHERO. Crown 8vo. Maps, 9s.

History of England un- der the Duke of Buckingham and Charles I. 1624-1628. By S. R. GARDINER. 2 vols. 8vo. Maps, 24s.

The Personal Govern- ment of Charles I. from the Death of Buckingham to the Declaration in favour of Ship Money, 1628-1637. By S. R. GARDINER. 2 vols. 8vo. 24s.

Popular History of France, from the Earliest Times to the Death of Louis XIV. By ELIZA-BETH M. SEWELL. With 8 Maps. Crown 8vo. 7s. 6d.

The Famine Campaign in Southern India, (Madras, Bombay, and Mysore,) in 1876-78. By WIL-LIAM DIGBY, Secretary of the Madras Famine Committee. With Maps and many Illustrations. 2 vols. 8vo. 32s.

A Student's Manual of the History of India from the Earliest Period to the Present. By Col. MEADOWS TAYLOR, M.R.A.S. Third Thousand. Crown 8vo. Maps, 7s. 6d.

Indian Polity; a View of the System of Administration in India. By Lieut.-Col. G. CHESNEY. 8vo. 21s.

Waterloo Lectures; a Study of the Campaign of 1815. By Colonel C. C. CHESNEY, R.E. 8vo. 10s. 6d.

The Oxford Reformers— John Colet, Erasmus, and Thomas More; a History of their Fellow-Work. By F. SEEBOHM. 8vo. 14s.

General History of Rome from B.C. 753 to A.D. 476. By Dean MERIVALE, D.D. Crown 8vo. Maps, price 7s. 6d.

The Fall of the Roman Republic; a Short History of the Last Century of the Commonwealth. By Dean MERIVALE, D.D. 12mo. 7s. 6d.

Carthage and the Cartha- ginians. By R. BOSWORTH SMITH, M.A. With 11 Maps, Plans & Illus-trations. Crown 8vo. 10s. 6d.

History of the Romans under the Empire. By Dean MERI-VALE, D.D. 8 vols. post 8vo. 48s.

The History of Rome. By WILHELM IHNE. VOLS. I. to III. 8vo. price 45s.

History of the Mongols from the Ninth to the Nineteenth Century. By HENRY H. HOWORTH, F.S.A. VOL. I. Royal 8vo. 28s.

The Sixth Oriental Mo-
narchy ; or, the Geography, History, and Antiquities of Parthia. By G. RAWLINSON, M.A. With Maps and Illustrations. 8vo. 16s.

The Seventh Great Ori-
ental Monarchy ; or, a History of the Sassanians. By G. RAWLINSON, M.A. With Map and 95 Illustrations. 8vo. 28s.

The History of European
Morals from Augustus to Charlemagne. By W. E. H. LECKY, M.A. 2 vols. crown 8vo. 16s.

History of the Rise and
Influence of the Spirit of Rationalism in Europe. By W. E. H. LECKY, M.A. 2 vols. crown 8vo. 16s.

The Childhood of the
English Nation; or, the Beginnings of English History. By ELLA S. ARMITAGE. Fcp. 8vo. 2s. 6d.

Sketch of the History of
the Church of England to the Revolution of 1688. By T. V. SHORT, D.D. Crown 8vo. 7s. 6d.

The History of Philo-
sophy, from Thales to Comte. By GEORGE HENRY LEWES. Fourth Edition 2 vols. 8vo. 32s.

Introduction to the Sci-
ence of Religion, Four Lectures delivered at the Royal Institution ; with Two Essays on False Analogies and the Philosophy of Mythology. By MAX MÜLLER, M.A. Crown 8vo. 10s. 6d.

Zeller's Stoics, Epicu-
reans, and Sceptics. Translated by the Rev. O. J. REICHEL, M.A. Cr. 8vo. 14s.

Zeller's Socrates & the
Socratic Schools. Translated by the Rev. O. J. REICHEL, M.A. Second Edition. Crown 8vo. 10s. 6d.

Zeller's Plato & the Older
Academy. Translated by S. FRANCES ALLEYNE and ALFRED GOODWIN, B.A. Crown 8vo. 18s.

Epochs of Modern His-
tory. Edited by C. COLBECK, M.A.

Church's Beginning of the Middle Ages, 2s. 6d.

Cox's Crusades, 2s. 6d.

Creighton's Age of Elizabeth, 2s. 6d.

Gairdner's Houses of Lancaster and York, 2s. 6d.

Gardiner's Puritan Revolution, 2s. 6d.

———— Thirty Years' War, 2s. 6d.

Hale's Fall of the Stuarts, 2s. 6d.

Johnson's Normans in Europe, 2s. 6d.

Ludlow's War of American Independence, 2s. 6d.

Morris's Age of Anne, 2s. 6d.

Seebohm's Protestant Revolution, price 2s. 6d.

Stubbs's Early Plantagenets, 2s. 6d.

Warburton's Edward III. 2s. 6d.

Epochs of Ancient His-
tory. Edited by the Rev. Sir G. W. COX, Bart. M.A. & C. SANKEY, M.A.

Beesly's Gracchi, Marius & Sulla, 2s.6d.

Capes's Age of the Antonines, 2s. 6d.

———— Early Roman Empire, 2s. 6d.

Cox's Athenian Empire, 2s. 6d.

- Greeks & Persians, 2s. 6d.

Curteis's Macedonian Empire, 2s. 6d.

Ihne's Rome to its Capture by the Gauls, 2s. 6d.

Merivale's Roman Triumvirates, 2s. 6d.

Sankey's Spartan & Theban Supremacies, 2s. 6d.

Epochs of English His-
tory. Edited by the Rev. MANDELL CREIGHTON, M.A.

Browning's Modern England, 1820-1874, 9d.

Cordery's Struggle against Absolute Monarchy, 1603-1688, 9d.

Creighton's (Mrs.) England a Continental Power, 1066-1216, 9d.

Creighton's (Rev. M.) Tudors and the Reformation, 1485 1603, 9d.

Rowley's Rise of the People, 1215-1485, 9d.

Rowley's Settlement of the Constitution, 1688-1778, 9d.

Tancock's England during the American & European Wars, 1778-1820, 9d.

York-Powell's Early England to the Conquest, 1s.

The Student's Manual of

Modern History; the Rise and Progress of the Principal European Nations. By W. COOKE TAYLOR, LL.D. Crown 8vo. 7s. 6d.

The Student's Manual of

Ancient History; the Political History, Geography and Social State of the Principal Nations of Antiquity. By W. COOKE TAYLOR, LL.D. Cr. 8vo. 7s. 6d.

BIOGRAPHICAL WORKS.

Memoirs of the Life of

Anna Jameson, Author of 'Sacred and Legendary Art' &c. By her Niece, GERARDINE MACPHERSON. 8vo. with Portrait, price 12s. 6d.

Memorials of Charlotte

Williams-Wynn. Edited by her Sister. Crown 8vo. with Portrait, price 10s. 6d.

The Life and Letters of

Lord Macaulay. By his Nephew, G. OTTO TREVELYAN, M.P.

CABINET EDITION, 2 vols. crown 8vo. 12s.
LIBRARY EDITION, 2 vols. 8vo. 36s.

The Life of Sir William

Fairbairn, Bart. F.R.S. Crown 8vo. 2s. 6d. demy 8vo. 18s.

The Life of Sir Martin

Frobisher, Knt. containing a Narrative of the Spanish Armada. By the Rev. FRANK JONES, B.A. Portrait, Maps, and Facsimile. Crown 8vo. 6s.

Arthur Schopenhauer, his

Life and his Philosophy. By HELEN ZIMMERN. Post 8vo. Portrait, 7s. 6d.

Gotthold Ephraim Les-

sing, his Life and Works. By HELEN ZIMMERN. Crown 8vo. 10s. 6d.

The Life, Works, and

Opinions of Heinrich Heine. By WILLIAM STIGAND. 2 vols. 8vo. Portrait, 28s.

The Life of Mozart.

Translated from the German Work of Dr. LUDWIG NOHL by Lady WALLACE. 2 vols. crown 8vo. 21s.

Life of Robert Frampton,

D.D. Bishop of Gloucester, deprived as a Non-Juror in 1689. Edited by T. S. EVANS, M.A. Crown 8vo. 10s. 6d.

Felix Mendelssohn's Let-

ters, translated by Lady WALLACE. 2 vols. crown 8vo. 5s. each.

Autobiography. By JOHN

STUART MILL. 8vo. 7s. 6d.

Apologia pro Vitâ Suâ;

Being a History of his Religious Opinions by JOHN HENRY NEWMAN, D.D. of the Oratory of St. Philip Neri. New Edition. Crown 8vo. 6s.

Pope Pius IX. By the

late J. F. MAGUIRE, M.P. Revised and brought down to the Accession of Pope Leo the Thirteenth by the Right Rev. Monsignor PATTERSON. Crown 8vo. Portraits, 6s. post 8vo. 2s. 6d.

Isaac Casaubon, 1559-

1614. By MARK PATTISON, Rector of Lincoln College, Oxford. 8vo. 18s.

Leaders of Public Opi-

nion in Ireland; Swift, Flood, Grattan, O'Connell. By W. E. H. LECKY, M.A. Crown 8vo. 7s. 6d.

Essays in Ecclesiastical

Biography. By the Right Hon. Sir J. STEPHEN, LL.D. Crown 8vo. 7s. 6d.

Dictionary of General

Biography; containing Concise Memoirs and Notices of the most Eminent Persons of all Ages and Countries. By W. L. R. CATES. 8vo. 25s.

Life of the Duke of Wel-

lington. By the Rev. G. R. GLEIG, M.A. Crown 8vo. Portrait, 6s.

Memoirs of Sir Henry

Havelock, K.C.B. By JOHN CLARK MARSHMAN. Crown 8vo. 3s. 6d.

Vicissitudes of Families.

By Sir BERNARD BURKE, C.B. Two vols. crown 8vo. 21s.

MENTAL and POLITICAL PHILOSOPHY.

Comte's System of Positive Polity, or Treatise upon Sociology :—

VOL. I. **General View of Positivism** and Introductory Principles. Translated by J. H. BRIDGES, M.B. 8vo. 21*s*.

VOL. II. **The Social Statics,** or the Abstract Laws of Human Order. Translated by F. HARRISON, M.A. 8vo. 14*s*.

VOL. III. **The Social Dynamics,** or the General Laws of Human Progress (the Philosophy of History). Translated by E. S. BEESLY, M.A. 8vo. 21*s*.

VOL. IV. **The Theory of the Future of Man;** with COMTE'S Early Essays on Social Philosophy. Translated by R. CONGREVE, M.D. and H. D. HUTTON, B.A. 8vo. 24*s*.

De Tocqueville's Democracy in America, translated by H. REEVE. 2 vols. crown 8vo. 16*s*.

Analysis of the Phenomena of the Human Mind. By JAMES MILL. With Notes, Illustrative and Critical. 2 vols. 8vo. 28*s*.

On Representative Government. By JOHN STUART MILL. Crown 8vo. 2*s*.

On Liberty. By JOHN STUART MILL. Post 8vo. 7*s*. 6*d*. crown 8vo. 1*s*. 4*d*.

Principles of Political Economy. By JOHN STUART MILL. 2 vols. 8vo. 30*s*. or 1 vol. crown 8vo. 5*s*.

Essays on some Unsettled Questions of Political Economy. By JOHN STUART MILL. 8vo. 6*s*. 6*d*.

Utilitarianism. By JOHN STUART MILL. 8vo. 5*s*.

The Subjection of Women. By JOHN STUART MILL. Fourth Edition. Crown 8vo. 6*s*.

Examination of Sir William Hamilton's Philosophy. By JOHN STUART MILL. 8vo. 16*s*.

A System of Logic, Ratiocinative and Inductive. By JOHN STUART MILL. 2 vols. 8vo. 25*s*.

Dissertations and Discussions. By JOHN STUART MILL. 4 vols. 8vo. price £2. 6*s*. 6*d*.

The Philosophy of Reflection. By SHADWORTH H. HODGSON, Hon. LL.D. Edin. Author of 'Time and Space,' and 'The Theory of Practice.' 2 vols. 8vo. 21*s*.

The Law of Nations considered as Independent Political Communities. By Sir TRAVERS TWISS, D.C.L. 2 vols. 8vo. £1. 13*s*.

A Systematic View of the Science of Jurisprudence. By SHELDON AMOS, M.A. 8vo. 18*s*.

A Primer of the English Constitution and Government. By S. AMOS, M.A. Crown 8vo. 6*s*.

A Sketch of the History of Taxes in England from the Earliest Times to the Present Day. By STEPHEN DOWELL. VOL. I. to the Civil War 1642. 8vo. 10*s*. 6*d*.

Principles of Economical Philosophy. By H. D. MACLEOD, M.A. Second Edition in 2 vols. VOL. I. 8vo. 15*s*. VOL. II. PART 1. 12*s*.

The Institutes of Justinian; with English Introduction, Translation, and Notes. By T. C. SANDARS, M.A. 8vo. 18*s*.

Lord Bacon's Works, collected & edited by R. L. ELLIS, M.A. J. SPEDDING, M.A. and D. D. HEATH. 7 vols. 8vo. £3. 13*s*. 6*d*.

Letters and Life of Francis Bacon, including all his Occasional Works. Collected and edited, with a Commentary, by J. SPEDDING. 7 vols. 8vo. £4. 4*s*.

The Nicomachean Ethics of Aristotle, translated into English by R. WILLIAMS, B.A. Crown 8vo. price 7*s*. 6*d*.

Aristotle's Politics, Books
I. III. IV. (VII.) Greek Text, with an English Translation by W. E. BOLLAND, M.A. and Short Essays by A. LANG, M.A. Crown 8vo. 7s. 6d.

The Politics of Aristotle;
Greek Text, with English Notes. By RICHARD CONGREVE, M.A. 8vo. 18s.

The Ethics of Aristotle;
with Essays and Notes. By Sir A. GRANT, Bart. LL.D. 2 vols. 8vo. 32s.

Bacon's Essays, with An-
notations. By R. WHATELY, D.D. 8vo. 10s. 6d.

Picture Logic; an Attempt
to Popularise the Science of Reasoning. By A. SWINBOURNE, B.A. Post 8vo. 5s.

Elements of Logic. By
R. WHATELY, D.D. 8vo. 10s. 6d. Crown 8vo. 4s. 6d.

Elements of Rhetoric.
By R. WHATELY, D.D. 8vo. 10s. 6d. Crown 8vo. 4s. 6d.

On the Influence of Au-
thority in Matters of Opinion. By the late Sir. G. C. LEWIS, Bart. 8vo. 14s.

The Senses and the In-
tellect. By A. BAIN, LL.D. 8vo. 15s.

The Emotions and the
Will. By A. BAIN, LL.D. 8vo. 15s.

Mental and Moral Sci-
ence; a Compendium of Psychology and Ethics. By A. BAIN, LL.D. Crown 8vo. 10s. 6d. Or separately, PART I. Mental Science, 6s. 6d. PART II. Moral Science, 4s. 6d.

An Outline of the Neces-
sary Laws of Thought; a Treatise on Pure and Applied Logic. By W. THOMPSON, D.D. Crown 8vo. 6s.

Hume's   Philosophical
Works. Edited, with Notes, &c. by T. H. GREEN, M.A. and the Rev. T. H. GROSE, M.A. 4 vols. 8vo. 56s. Or separately, Essays, 2 vols. 28s. Treatise on Human Nature, 2 vols. 28s.

The Schools of Charles
the Great, and the Restoration of Education in the Ninth Century. By J. BASS MULLINGER, M.A. 8vo. price 7s. 6d.

MISCELLANEOUS & CRITICAL WORKS.

The London Series of
English Classics. Edited by JOHN W. Hales, M.A. and by CHARLES S. JERRAM, M.A. Fcp. 8vo.

Bacon's Essays, annotated by E. A. ABBOT, D.D. 2 vols. 6s.

Ben Jonson's Every Man in His Humour, by H. B. WHEATLEY, F.S.A. Price 2s. 6d.

Macaulay's Clive, by H. C. BOWEN, M.A. 2s. 6d.

Marlowe's Doctor Faustus, by W. WAGNER, Ph.D. 2s.

Milton's Paradise Regained, by C. S. JERRAM, M.A. 2s. 6d.

Pope's Select Poems, by T. ARNOLD, M.A. 2s. 6d.

Miscellaneous Writings
of J. Conington, M.A. Edited by J. A. SYMONDS, M.A. 2 vols. 8vo. 28s.

Mesmerism, Spiritualism
&c. Historically and Scientifically Considered. By W. B. CARPENTER, F.R.S. &c. Crown 8vo. 5s.

Evenings with the Skep-
tics; or, Free Discussion on Free Thinkers. By JOHN OWEN, Rector of East Anstey, Devon. Crown 8vo. [*Just ready.*

Short Studies on Great
Subjects. By J. A. FROUDE, M.A. 3 vols. crown 8vo. 18s.

Manual of English Lite-
rature, Historical and Critical. By T. ARNOLD, M.A. Crown 8vo. 7s. 6d.

Lord Macaulay's Miscellaneous Writings :—

LIBRARY EDITION, 2 vols. 8vo. 21s.
PEOPLE'S EDITION, 1 vol. cr. 8vo. 4s. 6d.

Lord Macaulay's Miscellaneous Writings and Speeches.

Student's Edition. Crown 8vo. 6s.

Speeches of the Right

Hon. Lord Macaulay, corrected by Himself. Crown 8vo. 3s. 6d.

Selections from the Writings of Lord Macaulay.

Edited, with Notes, by G. O. TREVELYAN, M.P. Crown. 8vo. 6s.

The Rev. Sydney Smith's

Essays. Crown 8vo. 3s. 6d. cloth.

The Wit and Wisdom of

the Rev. Sydney Smith. Crown 8vo. 3s. 6d.

Miscellaneous and Post-

humous Works of the late Henry Thomas Buckle. Edited by HELEN TAYLOR. 3 vols. 8vo. 52s. 6d.

Miscellaneous Works of

Thomas Arnold, D.D. late Head Master of Rugby School. 8vo. 7s. 6d.

German Home Life ; a

Series of Essays on the Domestic Life of Germany. Crown 8vo. 6s.

Realities of Irish Life.

By W. STEUART TRENCH. Crown 8vo. 2s. 6d. sewed, or 3s. 6d. cloth.

Church and State ; their

Relations Historically Developed. By H. GEFFCKEN, Prof. of International Law, Univ. of Strasburg. Translated by E. F. TAYLOR. 2 vols. 8vo. 42s.

Lectures on the Science

of Language. By F. MAX MÜLLER, M.A. 2 vols. crown 8vo. 16s.

Chips from a German

Workshop ; Essays on the Science of Religion, and on Mythology, Traditions & Customs. By F. MAX MÜLLER, M.A. 4 vols. 8vo. £2. 18s.

Language & Languages.

A Revised Edition of Chapters on Language and Families of Speech. By F. W. FARRAR, D.D. F.R.S. Crown 8vo. 6s.

The Essays and Contri-

butions of A. K. H. B. Uniform Cabinet Editions in crown 8vo.

Recreations of a Country Parson, Three Series, 3s. 6d. each.

Landscapes, Churches, and Moralities, price 3s. 6d.

Seaside Musings, 3s. 6d.

Changed Aspects of Unchanged Truths, 3s. 6d.

Counsel and Comfort from a City Pulpit, 3s. 6d.

Lessons of Middle Age, 3s. 6d.

Leisure Hours in Town, 3s. 6d.

Autumn Holidays of a Country Parson, price 3s. 6d.

Sunday Afternoons at the Parish Church of a University City, 3s. 6d.

The Commonplace Philosopher in Town and Country, 3s. 6d.

Present-Day Thoughts, 3s. 6d.

Critical Essays of a Country Parson, price 3s. 6d.

The Graver Thoughts of a Country Parson, Three Series, 3s. 6d. each.

DICTIONARIES and OTHER BOOKS of REFERENCE.

Dictionary of the English

Language. By R. G. LATHAM, M.A. M.D. Abridged from Dr. Latham's Edition of Johnson's English Dictionary. Medium 8vo. 24s.

A Dictionary of the Eng-

lish Language. By R. G. LATHAM, M.A. M.D. Founded on Johnson's English Dictionary as edited by the Rev. H. J. TODD. 4 vols. 4to. £7.

Thesaurus of English
Words and Phrases, classified and arranged so as to facilitate the expression of Ideas, and assist in Literary Composition. By P. M. ROGET, M.D. Crown 8vo. 10s. 6d.

English Synonymes. By
E. J. WHATELY. Edited by R. WHATELY, D.D. Fcp. 8vo. 3s.

Handbook of the English
Language. By R. G. LATHAM, M.A. M.D. Crown 8vo. 6s.

Contanseau's Practical
Dictionary of the French and English Languages. Post 8vo. price 7s. 6d.

Contanseau's Pocket
Dictionary, French and English, abridged from the Practical Dictionary by the Author. Square 18mo. 3s. 6d.

A New Pocket Diction-
ary of the German and English Languages. By F. W. LONGMAN, Ball. Coll. Oxford. Square 18mo. 5s.

A Practical Dictionary
of the German and English Languages. By Rev. W. L. BLACKLEY, M.A. & Dr. C. M. FRIEDLÄNDER. Post 8vo. 7s. 6d.

A Dictionary of Roman
and Greek Antiquities. With 2,000 Woodcuts illustrative of the Arts and Life of the Greeks and Romans. By A. RICH, B.A. Crown 8vo. 7s. 6d.

The Critical Lexicon and
Concordance to the English and Greek New Testament. By the Rev. E. W. BULLINGER. Medium 8vo. 30s.

A Greek-English Lexi-
con. By H. G. LIDDELL, D.D. Dean of Christchurch, and R. SCOTT, D.D. Dean of Rochester. Crown 4to. 36s.

Liddell & Scott's Lexi-
con, Greek and English, abridged for Schools. Square 12mo. 7s. 6d.

An English-Greek Lexi-
con, containing all the Greek Words used by Writers of good authority. By C. D. YONGE, M.A. 4to. 21s.

Mr. Yonge's Lexicon,
English and Greek, abridged from his larger Lexicon. Square 12mo. 8s. 6d.

A Latin-English Diction-
ary. By JOHN T. WHITE, D.D. Oxon. and J. E. RIDDLE, M.A. Oxon. Sixth Edition, revised. 1 vol. 4to. 28s.

White's College Latin-
English Dictionary, for the use of University Students. Medium 8vo. 15s.

A Latin-English Diction-
ary for the use of Middle-Class Schools. By JOHN T. WHITE, D.D. Oxon. Square fcp. 8vo. 3s.

White's Junior Student's
Latin-English and English-Latin Dictionary. Square 12mo.

ENGLISH-LATIN DICTIONARY, 5s. 6d. LATIN-ENGLISH DICTIONARY, 7s. 6d. COMPLETE, 12s.

M'Culloch's Dictionary
of Commerce and Commercial Navigation. Re-edited by HUGH G. REID, Assistant-Comptroller H.H. Stationery Office. With 11 Maps and 30 Charts. 8vo. 63s.

Keith Johnston's General
Dictionary of Geography, Descriptive, Physical, Statistical, and Historical; a complete Gazetteer of the World. Medium 8vo. 42s.

The Public Schools Atlas
of Ancient Geography, in 28 entirely new Coloured Maps. Edited by the Rev. G. BUTLER, M.A. Imperial 8vo. or imperial 4to. 7s. 6d.

The Public Schools Atlas
of Modern Geography, in 31 entirely new Coloured Maps. Edited by the Rev. G. BUTLER, M.A. Imperial 8vo. or imperial 4to. 5s.

ASTRONOMY and METEOROLOGY.

Outlines of Astronomy.
By Sir J. F. W. HERSCHEL, Bart. M.A. Latest Edition, with Plates and Diagrams. Square crown 8vo. 12s.

Essays on Astronomy.
A Series of Papers on Planets and Meteors, the Sun and Sun-surrounding Space, Star and Star Cloudlets. By R. A. PROCTOR, B.A. With 10 Plates and 24 Woodcuts. 8vo. 12s.

The Moon; her Motions,
Aspects, Scenery, and Physical Condition. By R. A. PROCTOR, B.A. With Plates, Charts, Woodcuts, and Lunar Photographs. Crown 8vo. 10s. 6d.

The Sun; Ruler, Light, Fire,
and Life of the Planetary System. By R. A. PROCTOR, B.A. With Plates & Woodcuts. Crown 8vo. 14s.

The Orbs Around Us;
a Series of Essays on the Moon & Planets, Meteors & Comets, the Sun & Coloured Pairs of Suns. By R. A. PROCTOR, B.A. With Chart and Diagrams. Crown 8vo. 7s. 6d.

Other Worlds than Ours;
The Plurality of Worlds Studied under the Light of Recent Scientific Researches. By R. A. PROCTOR, B.A. With 14 Illustrations. Cr. 8vo. 10s. 6d.

The Universe of Stars;
Presenting Researches into and New Views respecting the Constitution of the Heavens. By R. A. PROCTOR, B.A. Second Edition, with 22 Charts (4 Coloured) and 22 Diagrams. 8vo. price 10s. 6d.

The Transits of Venus;
A Popular Account of Past and Coming Transits. By R. A. PROCTOR, B.A. 20 Plates (12 Coloured) and 27 Woodcuts. Crown 8vo. 8s. 6d.

Saturn and its System.
By R. A. PROCTOR, B.A. 8vo. with 14 Plates, 14s.

The Moon, and the Condition and Configurations of its Surface.
By E. NEISON, F.R.A.S. With 26 Maps & 5 Plates. Medium 8vo. 31s. 6d.

Celestial Objects for Common Telescopes.
By T. W. WEBB, M.A. With Chart and Woodcuts. New Edition in the press.

A New Star Atlas, for the
Library, the School, and the Observatory, in 12 Circular Maps (with 2 Index Plates). By R. A. PROCTOR, B.A. Crown 8vo. 5s.

Larger Star Atlas, for the
Library, in Twelve Circular Maps, with Introduction and 2 Index Plates. By R. A. PROCTOR, B.A. Folio, 15s. or Maps only, 12s. 6d.

Dove's Law of Storms,
considered in connexion with the Ordinary Movements of the Atmosphere. Translated by R. H. SCOTT, M.A. 8vo. 10s. 6d.

Air and Rain; the Beginnings of a Chemical Climatology.
By R. A. SMITH, F.R.S. 8vo. 24s.

Air and its Relations to
Life, 1774-1874; a Course of Lectures delivered at the Royal Institution. By W. N. HARTLEY, F.C.S. With 66 Woodcuts. Small 8vo. 6s.

Schellen's Spectrum
Analysis, in its Application to Terrestrial Substances and the Physical Constitution of the Heavenly Bodies. Translated by JANE and C. LASSELL, with Notes by W. HUGGINS, LL.D. F.R.S. 8vo. Plates and Woodcuts, 28s.

A Treatise on the Cycloid,
and on all forms of Cycloidal Curves, and on the use of Cycloidal Curves in dealing with the Motions of Planets, Comets, &c. and of Matter projected from the Sun. By R. A. PROCTOR, B.A. With 161 Diagrams. Crown 8vo. 10s. 6d.

NATURAL HISTORY and PHYSICAL SCIENCE.

Professor Helmholtz'
Popular Lectures on Scientific Subjects. Translated by E. ATKINSON, F.C.S. With numerous Wood Engravings. 8vo. 12s. 6d.

Professor Helmholtz on
the Sensations of Tone, as a Physiological Basis for the Theory of Music. Translated by A. J. ELLIS, F.R.S. 8vo. 36s.

Ganot's Natural Philo-
sophy for General Readers and Young Persons; a Course of Physics divested of Mathematical Formulæ and expressed in the language of daily life. Translated by E. ATKINSON, F.C.S. Third Edition. Plates and Woodcuts. Crown 8vo. 7s. 6d.

Ganot's Elementary
Treatise on Physics, Experimental and Applied, for the use of Colleges and Schools. Translated and edited by E. ATKINSON, F.C.S. Eighth Edition. Plates and Woodcuts. Post 8vo. 15s.

Arnott's Elements of Phy-
sics or Natural Philosophy. Seventh Edition, edited by A. BAIN, LL.D. and A. S. TAYLOR, M.D. F.R.S. Crown 8vo. Woodcuts, 12s. 6d.

The Correlation of Phy-
sical Forces. By the Hon. Sir W. R. GROVE, F.R.S. &c. Sixth Edition, revised and augmented. 8vo. 15s.

Weinhold's Introduction
to Experimental Physics; including Directions for Constructing Physical Apparatus and for Making Experiments. Translated by B. LOEWY, F.R.A.S. With a Preface by G. C. FOSTER, F.R.S. 8vo. Plates & Woodcuts 31s. 6d.

A Treatise on Magnet-
ism, General and Terrestrial. By H. LLOYD, D.D. D.C.L. 8vo. 10s. 6d.

Elementary Treatise on
the Wave-Theory of Light. By H. LLOYD, D.D. D.C.L. 8vo. 10s. 6d.

Fragments of Science.
By JOHN TYNDALL, F.R.S. Latest Edition. Crown 8vo. 10s. 6d.

Heat a Mode of Motion.
By JOHN TYNDALL, F.R.S. Fifth Edition nearly ready.

Sound. By JOHN TYNDALL,
F.R.S. Third Edition, including Recent Researches on Fog-Signalling. Crown 8vo. price 10s. 6d.

Researches on Diamag-
netism and Magne-Crystallic Action; including Diamagnetic Polarity. By JOHN TYNDALL, F.R.S. With 6 Plates and many Woodcuts. 8vo. 14s.

Contributions to Mole-
cular Physics in the domain of Radiant Heat. By JOHN TYNDALL, F.R.S. Plates and Woodcuts. 8vo. 16s.

Six Lectures on Light,
delivered in America in 1872 and 1873. By JOHN TYNDALL, F.R.S. Second Edition. Portrait, Plate, and Diagrams. Crown 8vo. 7s. 6d.

Lessons in Electricity at
the Royal Institution, 1875-6. By JOHN TYNDALL, F.R.S. With 58 Woodcuts. Crown 8vo. 2s. 6d.

Notes of a Course of
Seven Lectures on Electrical Phenomena and Theories, delivered at the Royal Institution. By JOHN TYNDALL, F.R.S. Crown 8vo. 1s. sewed, or 1s. 6d. cloth.

Notes of a Course of Nine
Lectures on Light, delivered at the Royal Institution. By JOHN TYNDALL, F.R.S. Crown 8vo. 1s. sewed, or 1s. 6d. cloth.

Principles of Animal Me-
chanics. By the Rev. S. HAUGHTON, F.R.S. Second Edition. 8vo. 21s.

Text-Books of Science,

Mechanical and Physical, adapted for the use of Artisans and of Students in Public and Science Schools.   Small 8vo. with Woodcuts, &c.

Abney's Photography, 3*s.* 6*d.*

Anderson's Strength of Materials, 3*s.*6*d.*

Armstrong's Organic Chemistry, 3*s.* 6*d.*

Barry's Railway Appliances, 3*s.* 6*d.*

Bloxam's Metals, 3*s.* 6*d.*

Goodeve's Mechanics, 3*s.* 6*d.*

—— —— Mechanism, 3*s.* 6*d.*

Gore's Electro-Metallurgy, 6*s.*

Griffin's Algebra & Trigonometry, 3/6.

Jenkin's Electricity & Magnetism, 3/6.

Maxwell's Theory of Heat, 3*s.* 6*d.*

Merrifield's Technical Arithmetic, 3*s.* 6*d.*

Miller's Inorganic Chemistry, 3*s.* 6*d.*

Preece & Sivewright's Telegraphy, 3/6.

Shelley's Workshop Appliances, 3*s* 6*d.*

Thomé's Structural and Physiological Botany, 6*s.*

Thorpe's Quantitative Analysis, 4*s.* 6*d.*

Thorpe & Muir's Qualitative Analysis, price 3*s.* 6*d.*

Tilden's Systematic Chemistry, 3*s.* 6*d.*

Unwin's Machine Design, 3*s.* 6*d.*

Watson's Plane & Solid Geometry, 3/6.

Light Science for Leisure

Hours; Familiar Essays on Scientific Subjects, Natural Phenomena, &c. By R. A. PROCTOR, B.A. 2 vols. crown 8vo. 7*s.* 6*d.* each.

The Comparative Ana-

tomy and Physiology of the Vertebrate Animals. By RICHARD OWEN, F.R.S. With 1,472 Woodcuts. 3 vols. 8vo. £3. 13*s.* 6*d.*

Kirby and Spence's In-

troduction to Entomology, or Elements of the Natural History of Insects. Crown 8vo. 5*s.*

A Familiar History of

Birds. By E. STANLEY, D.D. Fcp. 8vo. with Woodcuts, 3*s.* 6*d.*

Homes without Hands;

a Description of the Habitations of Animals, classed according to their Principle of Construction. By the Rev. J. G. WOOD, M.A. With about 140 Vignettes on Wood. 8vo. 14*s.*

Wood's Strange Dwell-

ings; a Description of the Habitations of Animals, abridged from 'Homes without Hands.' With Frontispiece and 60 Woodcuts. Crown 8vo. 7*s.* 6*d.*

Wood's Insects at Home;

a Popular Account of British Insects, their Structure, Habits, and Transformations. With 700 Woodcuts. 8vo. 14*s.*

Wood's Insects Abroad;

a Popular Account of Foreign Insects, their Structure, Habits, and Transformations. With 700 Woodcuts. 8vo. 14*s.*

Wood's Out of Doors; a

Selection of Original Articles on Practical Natural History. With 6 Illustrations. Crown 8vo. 7*s.* 6*d.*

Wood's Bible Animals; a

description of every Living Creature mentioned in the Scriptures, from the Ape to the Coral. With 112 Vignettes. 8vo. 14*s.*

The Sea and its Living

Wonders. By Dr. G. HARTWIG. 8vo. with numerous Illustrations, price 10*s.* 6*d.*

Hartwig's Tropical

World. With about 200 Illustrations. 8vo. 10*s.* 6*d.*

Hartwig's Polar World;

a Description of Man and Nature in the Arctic and Antarctic Regions of the Globe. Chromoxylographs, Maps, and Woodcuts. 8vo. 10*s.* 6*d.*

Hartwig's Subterranean

World. With Maps and Woodcuts. 8vo. 10*s.* 6*d.*

Hartwig's Aerial World;

a Popular Account of the Phenomena and Life of the Atmosphere. Map, Chromoxylographs, Woodcuts. 8vo. price 10*s.* 6*d.*

Rocks Classified and De-
scribed. By BERNHARD VON COTTA. An English Translation, by P. H. LAWRENCE (with English, German, and French Synonymes), revised by the Author. Post 8vo. 14s.

The Geology of England
and Wales; a Concise Account of the Lithological Characters, Leading Fossils, and Economic Products of the Rocks. By H. B. WOODWARD, F.G.S. Crown 8vo. Map & Woodcuts, 14s.

Keller's Lake Dwellings
of Switzerland, and other Parts of Europe. Translated by JOHN E. LEE, F.S.A. F.G.S. New Edition, enlarged, with 206 Illustrations. 2 vols. royal 8vo. 42s.

The Primæval World of
Switzerland. By Professor OSWAL HEER, of the University of Zurich. Edited by JAMES HEYWOOD, M.A. F.R.S. With Map, 19 Plates, & 372 Woodcuts. 2 vols. 8vo. 28s.

The Puzzle of Life and
How it Has Been Put Together; a Short History of Praehistoric Vegetable and Animal Life on the Earth. By A. NICOLS, F.R.G S. With 12 Illustrations. Crown 8vo. 3s. 6d.

The Origin of Civilisa-
tion, and the Primitive Condition of Man; Mental and Social Condition of Savages. By Sir J. LUBBOCK, Bart. M.P. F.R.S. 8vo. Woodcuts, 18s.

The Ancient Stone Im-
plements, Weapons, and Ornaments of Great Britain. By JOHN EVANS, F.R.S. With 2 Plates and 476 Woodcuts. 8vo. 28s.

A Dictionary of Science,
Literature, and Art. Re-edited by the late W. T. BRANDE (the Author) and the Rev. Sir G. W. COX, Bart., M.A. 3 vols. medium 8vo. 63s.

The History of Modern
Music, a Course of Lectures delivered at the Royal Institution of Great Britain. By JOHN HULLAH, LL.D. 8vo. price 8s. 6d.

Dr. Hullah's 2d Course
of Lectures on the Transition Period of Musical History, from the Beginning of the 17th to the Middle of the 18th Century. 8vo. 10s. 6d.

Loudon's Encyclopædia
of Plants; comprising the Specific Character, Description, Culture, History, &c. of all the Plants found in Great Britain. With upwards of 12,000 Woodcuts. 8vo. 42s.

De Caisne & Le Maout's
System of Descriptive and Analytical Botany. Translated by Mrs. HOOKER; edited and arranged according to the English Botanical System, by J. D. HOOKER, M.D. With 5,500 Woodcuts. Imperial 8vo. 31s. 6d.

Hand-Book of Hardy
Trees, Shrubs, and Herbaceous Plants; containing Descriptions &c. of the Best Species in Cultivation. With 720 Original Woodcut Illustrations. By W. B. HEMSLEY. Medium 8vo. 12s.

The Rose Amateur's
Guide. By THOMAS RIVERS. Latest Edition. Fcp. 8vo. 4s. 6d.

CHEMISTRY and PHYSIOLOGY.

Miller's Elements of Che-
mistry, Theoretical and Practical. Re-edited, with Additions, by H. MACLEOD, F.C.S. 3 vols. 8vo.
PART I. CHEMICAL PHYSICS. 16s.
PART II. INORGANIC CHEMISTRY, 24s.
PART III. ORGANIC CHEMISTRY, New Edition in the press.

Animal Chemistry; or,
the Relations of Chemistry to Physiology and Pathology: a Manual for Medical Men and Scientific Chemists. By CHARLES T. KINGZETT, F.C.S. 8vo. price 18s.

A Dictionary of Chemistry and the Allied Branches of other Sciences.
By HENRY WATTS, F.C.S. assisted by eminent Scientific and Practical Chemists. 7 vols. medium 8vo. £10. 16s. 6d.

Supplementary Volume, completing the Record of Chemical Discovery to the year 1877. [*In the press.*

Select Methods in Chemical Analysis,
chiefly Inorganic. By WM. CROOKES, F.R.S. With 22 Woodcuts. Crown 8vo. 12s. 6d.

The History, Products, and Processes of the Alkali Trade,
including the most recent Improvements. By CHARLES T. KINGZETT, F.C.S. With 32 Woodcuts. 8vo. 12s.

Health in the House:
Twenty-five Lectures on Elementary Physiology in its Application to the Daily Wants of Man and Animals. By Mrs. BUCKTON. Crown 8vo. Woodcuts, 2s.

The FINE ARTS and ILLUSTRATED EDITIONS.

In Fairyland; Pictures
from the Elf-World. By RICHARD DOYLE. With a Poem by W. ALLINGHAM. With 16 coloured Plates, containing 36 Designs. Folio, 15s.

Lord Macaulay's Lays of
Ancient Rome. With Ninety Illustrations on Wood from Drawings by G. SCHARF. Fcp. 4to. 21s.

Miniature Edition of
Macaulay's Lays of Ancient Rome, with Scharf's 90 Illustrations reduced in Lithography. Imp. 16mo. 10s. 6d.

Moore's Lalla Rookh.
TENNIEL'S Edition, with 68 Woodcut Illustrations. Fcp. 4to. 21s.

Moore's Irish Melodies,
MACLISE'S Edition, with 161 Steel Plates. Super-royal 8vo. 21s.

Lectures on Harmony,
delivered at the Royal Institution. By G. A. MACFARREN. 8vo. 12s.

Sacred and Legendary Art.
By Mrs. JAMESON. 6 vols. square crown 8vo. price £5. 15s. 6d.

Jameson's Legends of the
Saints and Martyrs. With 19 Etchings and 187 Woodcuts. 2 vols. 31s. 6d.

Jameson's Legends of the
Monastic Orders. With 11 Etchings and 88 Woodcuts. 1 vol. 21s.

Jameson's Legends of the
Madonna. With 27 Etchings and 165 Woodcuts. 1 vol. 21s.

Jameson's History of the
Saviour, His Types and Precursors. Completed by Lady EASTLAKE. With 13 Etchings and 281 Woodcuts. 2 vols. 42s.

The Three Cathedrals
dedicated to St. Paul in London. By W. LONGMAN, F.S.A. With numerous Illustrations. Square crown 8vo. 21s.

The USEFUL ARTS, MANUFACTURES, &c.

The Art of Scientific Discovery.
By G. GORE, LL.D. F.R.S. Author of 'The Art of Electro-Metallurgy.' Crown 8vo. price 15s.

The Amateur Mechanics'
Practical Handbook; describing the different Tools required in the Workshop. By A. H. G. HOBSON. With 33 Woodcuts. Crown 8vo. 2s. 6d.

The Engineer's Valuing
Assistant. By H. D. HOSKOLD, Civil and Mining Engineer, 16 years Mining Engineer to the Dean Forest Iron Company. 8vo. 31s. 6d.

Industrial Chemistry; a
Manual for Manufacturers and for Colleges or Technical Schools; a Translation (by Dr. T. H. BARRY) of Stohmann and Engler's German Edition of PAYEN'S 'Précis de Chimie Industrielle;' with Chapters on the Chemistry of the Metals, &c. by B. H. PAUL, Ph.D. With 698 Woodcuts. Medium 8vo. 42s.

Gwilt's Encyclopædia of
Architecture, with above 1,600 Woodcuts. Revised and extended by W. PAPWORTH. 8vo. 52s. 6d.

Lathes and Turning, Sim-
ple, Mechanical, and Ornamental. By W. H. NORTHCOTT. Second Edition, with 338 Illustrations. 8vo. 18s.

Hints on Household
Taste in Furniture, Upholstery, and other Details. By C. L. EASTLAKE. Fourth Edition, with 100 Illustrations. Square crown 8vo. 14s.

Handbook of Practical
Telegraphy. By R. S. CULLEY, Memb. Inst. C.E. Seventh Edition. Plates & Woodcuts. 8vo. price 16s.

A Treatise on the Steam
Engine, in its various applications to Mines, Mills, Steam Navigation, Railways and Agriculture. By J. BOURNE, C.E. With Portrait, 37 Plates, and 546 Woodcuts. 4to. 42s.

Recent Improvements in
the Steam Engine. By J. BOURNE, C.E. Fcp. 8vo. Woodcuts, 6s.

Catechism of the Steam
Engine, in its various Applications. By JOHN BOURNE, C.E. Fcp. 8vo. Woodcuts, 6s.

Handbook of the Steam
Engine, a Key to the Author's Catechism of the Steam Engine. By J. BOURNE, C.E. Fcp. 8vo. Woodcuts, 9s.

Encyclopædia of Civil
Engineering, Historical, Theoretical, and Practical. By E. CRESY, C.E. With above 3,000 Woodcuts. 8vo. 42s.

Ure's Dictionary of Arts,
Manufactures, and Mines. Seventh Edition, re-written and enlarged by R. HUNT, F.R.S. assisted by numerous contributors. With 2,604 Woodcuts. 4 vols. medium 8vo. £7. 7s.

Practical Treatise on Me-
tallurgy. Adapted from the last German Edition of Professor KERL'S Metallurgy by W. CROOKES, F.R.S. &c. and E. RÖHRIG, Ph.D. 3 vols. 8vo. with 625 Woodcuts. £4. 19s.

The Theory of Strains in
Girders and similar Structures, with Observations on the application of Theory to Practice, and Tables of the Strength and other Properties of Materials. By B. B. STONEY, M.A. M. Inst. C.E. Royal 8vo. with 5 Plates and 123 Woodcuts, 36s.

Railways and Locomo-
tives; a Series of Lectures delivered at the School of Military Engineering, Chatham, in the year 1877. *Railways*, by JOHN WOLFE BARRY, M. Inst. C.E. *Locomotives*, by F. J. BRAMWELL, F.R.S. M. Inst. C.E. [*In the press.*

A Treatise on Mills and
Millwork. By the late Sir W. FAIRBAIRN, Bart. C.E. Fourth Edition, with 18 Plates and 333 Woodcuts. 1 vol. 8vo. 25s.

Useful Information for
Engineers. By the late Sir W. FAIRBAIRN, Bart. C.E. With many Plates and Woodcuts. 3 vols. crown 8vo. 31s. 6d.

The Application of Cast
and Wrought Iron to Building Purposes. By the late Sir W. FAIRBAIRN, Bart. C.E. With 6 Plates and 118 Woodcuts. 8vo. 16s.

Anthracen; its Constitution,
Properties, Manufacture, and Derivatives, including Artificial Alizarin, Anthrapurpurin, &c. with their Applications in Dyeing and Printing. By G. AUERBACH. Translated by W. CROOKES, F.R.S 8vo. 12s.

Practical Handbook of
Dyeing and Calico-Printing. By
W. CROOKES, F.R.S. &c. With
numerous Illustrations and specimens
of Dyed Textile Fabrics. 8vo. 42s.

Mitchell's Manual of
Practical Assaying. Fourth Edition,
revised, with the Recent Discoveries
incorporated, by W. CROOKES, F.R.S.
Crown 8vo. Woodcuts, 31s. 6d.

Loudon's Encyclopædia
of Gardening; the Theory and Practice of Horticulture, Floriculture, Arbori-
culture & Landscape Gardening. With
1,000 Woodcuts. 8vo. 21s.

Loudon's Encyclopædia
of Agriculture; the Laying-out, Improvement, and Management of Landed
Property; the Cultivation and Economy
of the Productions of Agriculture. With
1,100 Woodcuts. 8vo. 21s.

RELIGIOUS and MORAL WORKS.

An Exposition of the 39
Articles, Historical and Doctrinal. By
E. H. BROWNE, D.D. Bishop of Win-
chester. Eleventh Edition. 8vo. 16s.

A Commentary on the
39 Articles, forming an Introduction to
the Theology of the Church of England.
By the Rev. T. P. BOULTBEE, LL.D.
New Edition. Crown 8vo. 6s.

Historical Lectures on
the Life of Our Lord Jesus Christ.
By C. J. ELLICOTT, D.D. 8vo. 12s.

Sermons preached most-
ly in the Chapel of Rugby School
by the late T. ARNOLD, D.D. Collective
Edition, revised by the Author's
Daughter, Mrs.W. E. FORSTER. 6 vols.
crown 8vo. 30s. or separately, 5s. each.

The Eclipse of Faith ; or
a Visit to a Religious Sceptic. By
HENRY ROGERS. Fcp. 8vo. 5s.

Defence of the Eclipse of
Faith. By H. ROGERS. Fcp. 8vo. 3s. 6d.

Nature, the Utility of
Religion and Theism. Three Essays
by JOHN STUART MILL. 8vo. 10s. 6d.

A Critical and Gram-
matical Commentary on St. Paul's
Epistles. By C. J. ELLICOTT, D.D.
8vo. Galatians, 8s. 6d. Ephesians,
8s. 6d. Pastoral Epistles, 10s. 6d.
Philippians, Colossians, & Philemon,
10s. 6d. Thessalonians, 7s. 6d.

Conybeare & Howson's
Life and Epistles of St. Paul.
Three Editions, copiously illustrated.

Library Edition, with all the Original
Illustrations, Maps, Landscapes on
Steel, Woodcuts, &c. 2 vols. 4to. 42s.

Intermediate Edition, with a Selection
of Maps, Plates, and Woodcuts. 2 vols.
square crown 8vo. 21s.

Student's Edition, revised and con-
densed, with 46 Illustrations and Maps.
1 vol. crown 8vo. 9s.

The Jewish Messiah ;
Critical History of the Messianic Idea
among the Jews, from the Rise of the
Maccabees to the Closing of the Tal-
mud. By JAMES DRUMMOND, B.A.
8vo. 15s.

Evidence of the Truth of
the Christian Religion derived from
the Literal Fulfilment of Prophecy. By
A. KEITH, D.D. 40th Edition, with
numerous Plates. Square 8vo. 12s. 6d.
or post 8vo. with 5 Plates, 6s.

The Prophets and Pro-
phecy in Israel; an Historical and
Critical Inquiry. By Prof. A. KUENEN,
Translated from the Dutch by the Rev.
A. MILROY, M.A. with an Introduc-
tion by J. MUIR, D.C.L. 8vo. 21s.

The History and Litera-
ture of the Israelites, according to
the Old Testament and the Apocrypha.
By C. DE ROTHSCHILD & A. DE
ROTHSCHILD. 2 vols. crown 8vo.
12s. 6d. 1 vol. fcp. 8vo. 3s. 6d.

Mythology among the
Hebrews and its Historical Development. By IGNAZ GOLDZIHER, Ph.D. Translated by RUSSELL MARTINEAU, M.A. 8vo. 16s.

Bible Studies. By M. M.
KALISCH, Ph.D. PART I. *The Prophecies of Balaam.* 8vo. 10s. 6d. PART II. *The Book of Jonah.* 8vo. 10s. 6d.

Historical and Critical
Commentary on the Old Testament; with a New Translation. By M. M. KALISCH, Ph.D. Vol. I. Genesis, 8vo. 18s. or adapted for the General Reader, 12s. Vol. II. Exodus, 15s. or adapted for the General Reader, 12s. Vol. III. Leviticus, Part I. 15s. or adapted for the General Reader, 8s. Vol. IV. Leviticus, Part II. 15s. or adapted for the General Reader, 8s.

Ewald's History of Israel.
Translated from the German by J. E. CARPENTER, M.A. with Preface by R. MARTINEAU, M.A. 5 vols. 8vo. 63s.

Ewald's Antiquities of
Israel. Translated from the German by H. S. SOLLY, M.A. 8vo. 12s. 6d.

The Trident, the Cres-
cent & the Cross; a View of the Religious History of India during the Hindu, Buddhist, Mohammedan, and Christian Periods. By the Rev. J. VAUGHAN. 8vo. 9s. 6d.

The Types of Genesis,
briefly considered as revealing the Development of Human Nature. By A. JUKES. Crown 8vo. 7s. 6d.

The Second Death and
the Restitution of all Things; with some Preliminary Remarks on the Nature and Inspiration of Holy Scripture. By A. JUKES. Crown 8vo. 3s. 6d.

History of the Reforma-
tion in Europe in the time of Calvin. By the Rev. J. H. MERLE D'AUBIGNÉ, D.D. Translated by W. L. R. CATES. 8 vols. 8vo. price £6. 12s.

Commentaries, by the Rev.
W. A. O'CONOR, B.A. Rector of St. Simon and St. Jude, Manchester.

Epistle to the Romans, crown 8vo. 3s. 6d.
Epistle to the Hebrews, 4s. 6d.
St. John's Gospel, 10s. 6d.

Supernatural Religion;
an Inquiry into the Reality of Divine Revelation. 3 vols. 8vo. 38s.

The Four Gospels in
Greek, with Greek-English Lexicon. By JOHN T. WHITE, D.D. Oxon. Square 32mo. 5s.

Passing Thoughts on
Religion. By ELIZABETH M. SEWELL. Fcp. 8vo. 3s. 6d.

Thoughts for the Age.
by ELIZABETH M. SEWELL. New Edition. Fcp. 8vo. 3s. 6d.

Preparation for the Holy
Communion; the Devotions chiefly from the works of Jeremy Taylor. By ELIZABETH M. SEWELL. 32mo. 3s.

The Ritual of the Altar,
or Order of the Holy Communion according to the Church of England. Edited by the Rev. O. SHIPLEY, M.A. Second Edition, revised and enlarged, with Frontispiece and 70 Woodcuts. Small folio, 42s.

Bishop Jeremy Taylor's
Entire Works; with Life by Bishop Heber. Revised and corrected by the Rev. C. P. EDEN. 10 vols. £5. 5s.

Hymns of Praise and
Prayer. Corrected and edited by Rev. JOHN MARTINEAU, LL.D. Crown 8vo. 4s. 6d. 32mo. 1s. 6d.

One Hundred Holy Songs,
Carols and Sacred Ballads, Original and Suitable for Music. Square fcp. 8vo. 2s. 6d.

Spiritual Songs for the
Sundays and Holidays throughout the Year. By J. S. B. MONSELL, LL.D. Fcp. 8vo. 5s. 18mo. 2s.

Lyra Germanica; Hymns

translated from the German by Miss C. WINKWORTH. Fcp. 8vo. 5s.

The Temporal Mission

of the Holy Ghost; or, Reason and Revelation. By HENRY EDWARD MANNING, D.D. Crown 8vo. 8s. 6d.

Hours of Thought on

Sacred Things; a Volume of Sermons. By JAMES MARTINEAU, D.D. LL.D. Crown 8vo. Price 7s. 6d.

Endeavours after the

Christian Life; Discourses. By JAMES MARTINEAU, D.D. LL.D. Fifth Edition. Crown 8vo. 7s. 6d.

The Pentateuch & Book

of Joshua Critically Examined. By J. W. COLENSO, D.D. Bishop of Natal. Crown 8vo. 6s.

Lectures on the Penta-

teuch and the Moabite Stone; with Appendices. By J. W. COLENSO, D.D. Bishop of Natal. 8vo. 12s.

TRAVELS, VOYAGES, &c.

A Voyage in the 'Sun-

beam,' our Home on the Ocean for Eleven Months. By Mrs. BRASSEY. Sixth Edition, with 8 Maps and Charts and 118 Wood Engravings. 8vo. 21s.

A Year in Western

France. By M. BETHAM-EDWARDS. Crown 8vo. Frontispiece, 10s. 6d.

One Thousand Miles up

the Nile; a Journey through Egypt and Nubia to the Second Cataract. By AMELIA B. EDWARDS. With Plans, Maps & Illustrations. Imperial 8vo. 42s.

The Indian Alps, and How

we Crossed them; Two Years' Residence in the Eastern Himalayas, and Two Months' Tour into the Interior. By a LADY PIONEER. With Illustrations. Imperial 8vo. 42s.

Discoveries at Ephesus,

Including the Site and Remains of the Great Temple of Diana. By J. T. WOOD, F.S.A. With 27 Lithographic Plates and 42 Wood Engravings. Medium 8vo. 63s.

Through Bosnia and the

Herzegovina on Foot during the Insurrection, August and September 1875. By ARTHUR J. EVANS, B.A. F.S.A. Map & Woodcuts. 8vo. 18s.

Illyrian Letters, from the

Provinces of Bosnia, Herzegovina, Montenegro, Albania, Dalmatia, Croatia & Slavonia, during the year 1877. By A. J. EVANS, B.A. F.S.A. Post 8vo. Maps. 7s. 6d.

Over the Sea and Far

Away; a Narrative of a Ramble round the World. By T. W. HINCH-LIFF, M.A. With 14 full-page Illustrations. Medium 8vo. 21s.

Guide to the Pyrenees,

for the use of Mountaineers. By CHARLES PACKE. Crown 8vo. 7s. 6d.

The Alpine Club Map of

Switzerland, with parts of the Neighbouring Countries, on the scale of Four Miles to an Inch. Edited by R. C. NICHOLS, F.R.G.S. 4 Sheets in Portfolio, 42s. coloured, or 34s. uncoloured.

The Alpine Guide. By

JOHN BALL, M.R.I.A. Post 8vo. with Maps and other Illustrations.

The Eastern Alps, 10s. 6d.

Central Alps, including all

the Oberland District, 7s. 6d.

Western Alps, including

Mont Blanc, Monte Rosa, Zermatt, &c. Price 6s. 6d.

On Alpine Travelling and

the Geology of the Alps. Price 1s. Either of the 3 Volumes or Parts of the 'Alpine Guide' may be had with this Introduction prefixed, 1s. extra. 'The Alpine Guide' may also be had in 10 separate Parts, or districts, 2s. 6d. each.

How to see Norway. By

J. R. CAMPBELL. Fcp. 8vo. Map & Woodcuts, 5s.

Memorials of the Discovery and Early Settlement of the Bermudas or Somers Islands,

from 1615 to 1685. By Major-General Sir J. H. LEFROY, R.A. Vol. I. imperial 8vo. with 2 Maps, 30s.

Eight Years in Ceylon.

By Sir SAMUEL W. BAKER, M.A. Crown 8vo. Woodcuts, 7s. 6d.

The Rifle and the Hound

in Ceylon. By Sir SAMUEL W. BAKER, M.A. Crown 8vo. Woodcuts, 7s. 6d.

WORKS of FICTION.

Novels and Tales. By the

Right Hon. the EARL of BEACONS-FIELD, K.G. Cabinet Editions, complete in Ten Volumes, crown 8vo. 6s. each.

Lothair, 6s.	Venetia, 6s.
Coningsby, 6s.	Alroy, Ixion, &c. 6s.
Sybil, 6s.	Young Duke &c. 6s.
Tancred, 6s.	Vivian Grey, 6s.
	Henrietta Temple, 6s.
	Contarini Fleming, &c. 6s.

The Atelier du Lys; or an

Art-Student in the Reign of Terror. By the author of 'Mademoiselle Mori.' Third Edition. Crown 8vo. 6s.

Whispers from Fairyland.

By the Right Hon. E. H. KNATCHBULL-HUGESSEN, M.P. With 9 Illustrations. Crown 8vo. 3s. 6d.

Higgledy-Piggledy; or,

Stories for Everybody and Everybody's Children. By the Right Hon. E. H. KNATCHBULL-HUGESSEN, M.P. With 9 Illustrations. Cr. 8vo. 3s. 6d.

Stories and Tales. By

ELIZABETH M. SEWELL. Cabinet Edition, in Ten Volumes, each containing a complete Tale or Story:—

Amy Herbert, 2s. 6d. Gertrude, 2s. 6d. The Earl's Daughter, 2s. 6d. The Experience of Life, 2s. 6d. Cleve Hall, 2s. 6d. Ivors, 2s. 6d. Katharine Ashton, 2s. 6d. Margaret Percival, 3s. 6d. Laneton Parsonage, 3s. 6d. Ursula, 3s. 6d.

The Modern Novelist's

Library. Each work complete in itself, price 2s. boards, or 2s. 6d. cloth.

By Lord BEACONSFIELD.

Lothair.
Coningsby.
Sybil.
Tancred.
Venetia.
Henrietta Temple.
Contarini Fleming.
Alroy, Ixion, &c.
The Young Duke, &c.
Vivian Grey.

By ANTHONY TROLLOPE.

Barchester Towers.
The Warden.

By the Author of 'The Rose Garden.'

Unawares.

By Major WHYTE-MELVILLE.

Digby Grand.
General Bounce.
Kate Coventry.
The Gladiators.
Good for Nothing.
Holmby House.
The Interpreter.
The Queen's Maries.

By the Author of 'The Atelier du Lys.'

Mademoiselle Mori.

By Various Writers.

Atherstone Priory.
The Burgomaster's Family.
Elsa and her Vulture.
The Six Sisters of the Valleys.

The Novels and Tales of the Right Honourable

the Earl of Beaconsfield, K.G. Complete in Ten Volumes, crown 8vo. cloth extra, gilt edges, price 30s.

POETRY and THE DRAMA.

Lays of Ancient Rome;
with Ivry and the Armada. By LORD MACAULAY. 16mo. 3s. 6d.

Horatii Opera. Library
Edition, with English Notes, Marginal References & various Readings. Edited by Rev. J. E. YONGE, M.A. 8vo. 21s.

Poems by Jean Ingelow.
2 vols. fcp. 8vo. 10s.

FIRST SERIES, containing 'Divided,' 'The Star's Monument,' &c. Fcp. 8vo. 5s.

SECOND SERIES, 'A Story of Doom,' 'Gladys and her Island,' &c.   5s.

Poems by Jean Ingelow.
First Series, with nearly 100 Woodcut Illustrations. Fcp. 4to. 21s.

Festus, a Poem. By
PHILIP JAMES BAILEY. 10th Edition, enlarged & revised. Crown 8vo. 12s. 6d.

The Iliad of Homer, Ho-
mometrically translated by C. B. CAYLEY, Translator of Dante's Comedy, &c. 8vo. 12s. 6d.

The Æneid of Virgil.
Translated into English Verse. By J. CONINGTON, M.A. Crown 8vo. 9s.

Bowdler's Family Shak-
speare. Genuine Edition, in 1 vol. medium 8vo. large type, with 36 Woodcuts, 14s. or in 6 vols. fcp. 8vo. 21s.

Southey's Poetical
Works, with the Author's last Corrections and Additions. Medium 8vo. with Portrait, 14s.

RURAL SPORTS, HORSE and CATTLE MANAGEMENT, &c.

Annals of the Road; or,
Notes on Mail and Stage-Coaching in Great Britain. By Captain MALET. With 3 Woodcuts and 10 Coloured Illustrations. Medium 8vo. 21s.

Down the Road; or, Re-
miniscences of a Gentleman Coachman. By C. T. S. BIRCH REYNARDSON. Second Edition, with 12 Coloured Illustrations. Medium 8vo. 21s.

Blaine's Encyclopædia of
Rural Sports; Complete Accounts, Historical, Practical, and Descriptive, of Hunting, Shooting, Fishing, Racing, &c. With 600 Woodcuts. 8vo. 21s.

A Book on Angling; or,
Treatise on the Art of Fishing in every branch; including full Illustrated Lists of Salmon Flies. By FRANCIS FRANCIS. Post 8vo. Portrait and Plates, 15s.

Wilcocks's Sea-Fisher-
man: comprising the Chief Methods of Hook and Line Fishing, a glance at Nets, and remarks on Boats and Boating. Post 8vo. Woodcuts, 12s. 6d.

The Fly-Fisher's Ento-
mology. By ALFRED RONALDS. With 20 Coloured Plates. 8vo. 14s.

Horses and Riding. By
GEORGE NEVILE, M.A. With 31 Illustrations. Crown 8vo. 6s.

Horses and Stables. By
Colonel F. FITZWYGRAM, XV. the King's Hussars. With 24 Plates of Illustrations. 8vo. 10s. 6d.

Youatt on the Horse.
Revised and enlarged by W. WATSON, M.R.C.V.S. 8vo. Woodcuts, 12s. 6d.

Youatt's Work on the
Dog. Revised and enlarged. 8vo. Woodcuts, 6s.

The Dog in Health and
Disease. By STONEHENGE. With 73 Wood Engravings. Square crown 8vo. 7s. 6d.

The Greyhound. By
STONEHENGE. Revised Edition, with 25 Portraits of Greyhounds, &c. Square crown 8vo. 15s.

Stables and Stable Fittings.
By W. MILES. Imp. Svo. with 13 Plates, 15s.

The Horse's Foot, and
How to keep it Sound. By W. MILES. Imp. 8vo. Woodcuts, 12s. 6d.

A Plain Treatise on
Horse-shoeing. By W. MILES. Post Svo. Woodcuts, 2s. 6d.

Remarks on Horses'
Teeth, addressed to Purchasers. By W. MILES. Post Svo. 1s. 6d.

The Ox, his Diseases and
their Treatment; with an Essay on Parturition in the Cow. By J. R. DOBSON, M.R.C.V.S. Crown Svo. Illustrations, 7s. 6d.

WORKS of UTILITY and GENERAL INFORMATION.

Maunder's Treasury of
Knowledge and Library of Reference; comprising an English Dictionary and Grammar, Universal Gazetteer, Classical Dictionary, Chronology, Law Dictionary, Synopsis of the Peerage, Useful Tables, &c. Fcp. Svo. 6s.

Maunder's Biographical
Treasury. Latest Edition, reconstructed and partly re-written, with above 1,600 additional Memoirs, by W. L. R. CATES. Fcp. Svo. 6s.

Maunder's Scientific and
Literary Treasury; a Popular Encyclopædia of Science, Literature, and Art. Latest Edition, partly re-written, with above 1,000 New Articles, by J. Y. JOHNSON. Fcp. Svo. 6s.

Maunder's Treasury of
Geography, Physical, Historical, Descriptive, and Political. Edited by W. HUGHES, F.R.G.S. With 7 Maps and 16 Plates. Fcp. Svo. 6s.

Maunder's Historical
Treasury; Introductory Outlines of Universal History, and Separate Histories of all Nations. Revised by the Rev. Sir G. W. Cox, Bart. M.A. Fcp. Svo. 6s.

Maunder's Treasury of
Natural History; or, Popular Dictionary of Zoology. Revised and corrected Edition. Fcp. Svo. with 900 Woodcuts, 6s.

The Treasury of Botany,
or Popular Dictionary of the Vegetable Kingdom; with which is incorporated a Glossary of Botanical Terms. Edited by J. LINDLEY, F.R.S. and T. MOORE, F.L.S. With 274 Woodcuts and 20 Steel Plates. Two Parts, fcp. Svo. 12s.

The Treasury of Bible
Knowledge; being a Dictionary of the Books, Persons, Places, Events, and other Matters of which mention is made in Holy Scripture. By the Rev. J. AYRE, M.A. Maps, Plates & Woodcuts. Fcp. Svo. 6s.

A Practical Treatise on
Brewing; with Formulæ for Public Brewers & Instructions for Private Families. By W. BLACK. Svo. 10s. 6d.

The Theory of the Modern Scientific Game of Whist.
By W. POLE, F.R.S. Tenth Edition. Fcp. Svo. 2s. 6d.

The Correct Card; or,
How to Play at Whist; a Whist Catechism. By Captain A. CAMPBELL-WALKER, F.R.G.S. New Edition. Fcp. Svo. 2s. 6d.

The Cabinet Lawyer; a
Popular Digest of the Laws of England, Civil, Criminal, and Constitutional. Twenty-Fifth Edition, corrected and extended. Fcp. Svo. 9s.

Chess Openings. By F.W.
LONGMAN, Balliol College, Oxford. Second Edition. Fcp. Svo. 2s. 6d.

English Chess Problems.
Edited by J. PIERCE, M.A. and W. T. PIERCE. With 608 Diagrams. Crown Svo. 12s. 6d.

Pewtner's Comprehensive Specifier;
a Guide to the Practical Specification of every kind of Building-Artificer's Work. Edited by W. YOUNG. Crown Svo. 6s.

A Handbook on Gold
and Silver. By an INDIAN OFFICER.
8vo. 12s. 6d.

The English Manual of
Banking. By ARTHUR CRUMP.
Second Edition, revised and enlarged.
8vo. 15s.

Modern Cookery for Pri-
vate Families, reduced to a System
of Easy Practice in a Series of carefully-
tested Receipts. By ELIZA ACTON.
With 8 Plates and 150 Woodcuts. Fcp.
8vo. 6s.

Hints to Mothers on the
Management of their Health during
the Period of Pregnancy and in the
Lying-in Room. By THOMAS BULL,
M.D. Fcp. 8vo, 2s. 6d.

The Maternal Manage-
ment of Children in Health and
Disease. By THOMAS BULL, M.D.
Fcp. 8vo. 2s. 6d.

Economics for Beginners
By H. D. MACLEOD, M.A. Small
crown 8vo. 2s. 6d.

The Elements of Bank-
ing. By H. D. MACLEOD, M.A.
Third Edition. Crown 8vo. 7s. 6d.

The Theory and Practice
of Banking. By H. D. MACLEOD,
M.A. 2 vols. 8vo. 26s.

The Resources of Mod-
ern Countries ; Essays towards an
Estimate of the Economic Position of
Nations and British Trade Prospects.
By ALEX. WILSON. 2 vols. 8vo. 24s.

Willich's Popular Tables
for ascertaining, according to the Carlisle
Table of Mortality, the value of Life-
hold, Leasehold, and Church Property,
Renewal Fines, Reversions, &c. Also
Interest, Legacy, Succession Duty, and
various other useful tables. Eighth
Edition. Post 8vo. 10s.

INDEX.

LONDON : PRINTED BY
SPOTTISWOODE AND CO., NEW-STREET SQUARE
AND PARLIAMENT STREET